Social Influence:
Attracting a Massive Following & Driving Organic Sales Using Social Media

By StartUp Mindset

STARTUP MINDSET

Copyright © 2018 StartUp Mindset, LLC

All rights reserved. No part of this publication may be reproduced, distributed, or transmitted in any form or by any means, including photocopying, recording, or other electronic or mechanical methods, without the prior written permission of the publisher, except in the case of brief quotations embodied in critical reviews and certain other noncommercial uses permitted by copyright law. For permission requests, write to the publisher, addressed "Attention: Permissions Coordinator," at the address below. All rights reserved.

DEDICATION

To the team at StartUp Mindset, the hundreds of thousands of readers, and you.

CONTENTS

1	Our first 100,000 Followers	5
2	The Language of Social Media	21
3	Getting Ready to Reach	47
4	Growing on Facebook	62
5	Growing on Instagram	82
6	Growing on Twitter	111
7	Connecting with LinkedIn	129
8	Beating Newsfeed Algorithms	136
9	Selling Through Story Telling	147
10	Selling Using Content	159
11	Writing Attention Getting Headlines	172
12	Using Influencers to Spike Your Growth	181
	Conclusion	192

CHAPTER 1
OUR FIRST 100,000 FOLLOWERS

"We're living at a time when attention is the new currency. Those who insert themselves into as many channels as possible look set to capture the most value."

-*Pete Cashmore, Founder of Mashable.com*

I remember thinking to myself that I'd be happy if StartUp Mindset reached 3,000 followers on Twitter. We already on Facebook and had been growing at a decent rate. I put all of my energy into trying to build a large Facebook following in those early days.

It was 2014 and I was still working in finance and was running my personal blog part-time. But since I had started online businesses before and had already validated the idea of StartUp Mindset, I put all of my energy into growing the following. I tested content, interacted with everyone who engaged with the page, and experimented with Facebook page boosts to gain visibility.

My hard work was paying off as we were growing at about 500-1,000 likes a month. This was awesome because Facebook was a known traffic driver and people on the platform seemed to be interested in StartUp Mindset and our business philosophy. Then things changed for the worse and it wouldn't be the last time.

Facebook made to decision to change their algorithm. This would be the first of many that would effect publishers and is still something we anticipate happening more frequently as the platform continues to mature. This particular change made it harder for me to reach the 5,000 or so followers that liked the page at that time.

I was still reaching about 80% of my audience so I was still satisfied with the engagement. But, I have always been someone who likes to look at what is coming, not what is here. I knew that more changes were coming and I needed a backup plan. I needed to not put all of my eggs in one basket and rely on one single referral source.

What are my options?

I first thought Twitter would be a good option. We already had the profile set up but if you were to see it you would have thought it was abandoned since the only tweet was several months old and read "StartUpmindset.com launching soon".

I also looked at Instagram, Pinterest, and social bookmarking sites such as StumbleUpon, Digg, and Reddit. From my personal blogging experience, those platforms had the power to drive a lot of traffic to any site if a piece of content caught fire. However, I doubted my ability to build my own community around those platforms (excluding Reddit).

I decided to go back to Twitter. It was the next logical choice for us since we would be sharing content frequently. So for a few weeks, I spent hours on Twitter. I began following people, tweeting motivational tweets and retweeting. The profile gained a few followers but nothing to get excited about. I still held on to the idea of using the platform but I didn't really know how to yet.

Launching the site and seeing the truth

Months later, we officially launched Startupmindet.com. Our Facebook fans loved it! We were not only sharing other informational articles but we also had our own points of view. The engagement was high and the following increased. We were still reaching 80% of our audience so I was satisfied with that. I even got a little comfortable with the idea of using Facebook as our primary traffic driver. Then, it happened again.

Facebook decreased our reach. I knew it was coming and that's when I saw the truth: algorithm changes are inevitable and I could never rely on one single platform. This means that anyone who wants to have a consistent pool of leads should never rely on just one source. Just like all good businesses diversify their revenue streams, you as an entrepreneur should not rely on a single referral source.

On StartUp Mindset, I had the opportunity to interview Susan Packard. Susan is the Cofounder of HGTV, the massively popular cable network that, in 2016, overtook CNN as the third most-watched cable channel in the United States behind Fox News and ESPN with an estimated reach 95,628,000 households.

Packard Co-founded Scripps Networks Interactive and they were responsible for starting and growing digital brands like HGTV and CNBC. Starting a cable network during the 1990's is comparable to starting an online media network today.

With everyone trying to get everyone else's attention, your strategy has to be stellar and your execution precise in order to come out on top. Many networks came and went during those times but a few of them had staying power. The networks developed by Susan and Scripps were among the few that did.

One of the keys she mentioned when launching the new network was communicating with your audience in as many ways as possible. That means being everywhere they are and knowing what is going on in their lives so that you can provide assistance or serve them in some way.

This was the same thing I realized with the whole Facebook algorithm slap-in-the-face. I knew that even if I couldn't duplicate the growth on Twitter, I should be diversifying our reach as well as having an alternative way of staying connected with our audience. Little did I know that not only would we recreate the hyper growth on Facebook, we would surpass it by several 1,000%.

The Road to 100,000

We announced that we were launching our Twitter profile in February of 2016 on our Facebook page. We noticed a few faithful Facebook followers came over to Twitter to follow us. But for the most part, we saw very little excitement around our Twitter launch. To be honest, I wasn't that excited either. I liked Twitter for personal use but really didn't see how we could stand out in any real way.

The early lack of enthusiasm our followers showed us by not joining us on Twitter did not help my skepticism. What I would learn later (and what you will learn later too in this book) is that just because your current followers don't rush to your other platforms doesn't mean they don't care about you. It just means that they don't want to leave their current platform.

When someone is using a social media app, they are expecting an experience. Even if they don't know what that experience is, they expect a certain level of satisfaction. When users of Instagram are scrolling through the images and stories, they are looking for visually appealing content. Trying to drive those users to Twitter which is largely text-based, is asking for a lot for a casual fan of your brand or business.

Convincing 8,000 people to leave their current platform in order to join another platform without incentive is ridiculous.

Most followers of a brand expect the brand to publish the same content across multiple platforms. I mean, why would I follow a platform that posts the same thing on across all of their feeds? It makes more sense to me pick one platform and follow there unless I know that I don't want to miss a discount, piece of content, or update.

Things changed for us when I realized that we needed to enter each platform as if we had no following at all. We had to learn the language of each platform and become a part of the DNA of each individual social media platform. We had to find out what worked for each.

Once that happened, we could keep building our audience until the new account had a personality of its own. We could then incentivize our other followers to join us on the adjacent platform for things they would not get on the current platform that they engaged with us on.

For example, we tweeted about 5 times per day on Twitter in the beginning. But what we shared on Twitter was different than what we shared on Facebook. We had polls, images, and more content. When we asked our followers to join us on Twitter, we added a screenshot of our feed and told them in the description of the things that we do on Twitter that we don't do often on Facebook.

That added some sense of intrigue to our Facebook feed since our followers on Facebook would see that Twitter is a whole other world. And if they liked us on Facebook, they would love us on Twitter.

Workin' it out on Twitter

Even though we did all we could to drive our followers from Facebook to Twitter, I knew it wouldn't be enough. I knew that we would have to work hard to make Twitter work for us. After all, not everyone that is on Facebook wants to be on Twitter and vice versa.

Later on in this book, we will tell you more about our Twitter strategy so we'll leave a lot of that information until then, but you should know that it was a daily commitment to engage on Twitter. At first, I spent 3, 4, and sometimes 5 hours a day interacting with people on the platform.

I made sure that I tweeted, retweeted, followed, and liked as much as I could. Once I got a system going, I was able to spend about 1 hour a day on the platform and would still see a spike in following and engagement.

Slowly the traffic started to increase, 3,000, 5,000, 8,500 and finally 10,000. I was stoked that we had finally reached 10,000 followers. And it wasn't slowing down. A few influential profiles retweeting our content and actively engaging pushed our following above 25,000.

The good news, then the bad news, and then the good news.

The good news was that our Twitter following had finally passed our Facebook following and there was no slowing us down. The bad news was we were not seeing a lot of traffic from Twitter. Not as much as what we expected. **But we were seeing something else; influence.**

The one thing about Twitter is the fact that you can connect with just about anyone. What we began to notice were the opportunities that came from the amount of reach we had. The reality was, just because we didn't get a click thru, didn't mean we weren't influencing.

At the time we were getting around 30,000-50,000 impressions per month. This was great for brand awareness. The more our brand was being viewed, the more our following increased. Being retweeted often by our followers helped us gain the attention of others. Of course, we had to make sure that what we posted was quality and worth checking out. It was crucial that we did not tarnish our reputation by being spammy.

Imagine your brand, logo, or product being seen 50,000 times a month...for free. That was the amazing thing about Twitter, **we spent $0 on Twitter ads**. Although I believed Twitter ads would help our brand awareness, I figured out a way to grow our following without having to utilize the tool.

The reach that we had helped us partner with other media outlets and I was asked to be interviewed on a few online podcasts. These opportunities would not have happened unless we dove straight into the Twitter world.

There were several other strategies we attempted during our climb to 100k. Some worked, some didn't. We will tell you some of what worked later in this book. The spike in Twitter following came at the right time as we continued to see a drop in Facebook reach. Our following on the platform also slowed. We had about 9,000 followers (we later learned that 9,000 followers was more than enough to maximize our business) and we were reaching less than 40% of them with each post.

Surprisingly, Facebook still brought in a decent amount of traffic even with the drop in reach. Building our Facebook following was definitely worth it. We still invest time in posting quality content on our page and the page continues to grow.

When our total following was over 100,000, I couldn't believe it. Around the 50,000 follower mark, I wanted to cross the 100k to see what impact it would make on our media business. Here are some things that happened on the way to 100,000 followers.

What happens when your following Increases

Attention-One of Gary Vaynerchuk's favorite phrases is "attention is the currency of business". In our case, this was absolutely true. When our following grew, the amount of attention we commanded grew. This reach allowed us to ask questions from more people and develop a better product (content) for them to consume.

If you are trying to sell a product or service and no one is buying, you must find out why. Having access to a large audience allows you to test and ask for valuable feedback. The more people in your following, the more diverse input you will receive. We also began getting attention from other media platforms.

Partnerships-Partnership opportunities with influential people and businesses began to present themselves. For example, one of the early partnerships that proved beneficial for both parties was our collaboration with SWAAY Media. The media platform was founded by Iman Oubou who was crowned Miss New York in 2015.

Along with being a pageant winner, Oubou is also a brilliant entrepreneur. She reached out to me in order to establish a syndication partnership that helped StartUp Mindset reach a new audience as we provided quality content for their platform.

Expanding our Team-When I first started StartUp Mindset I looked to build a team which is hard when you don't even have a viable business. Even finding writers for the site was difficult. With the increase in following and influence, we started getting approached by writers, administration assistants, and others wanting to join our team and what we were building.

Increased Revenue-StartUp Mindset was a bootstrapped startup meaning we did not take outside investments. I'm not a big believer in venture funding as a goal. So it was important that we were cashflow positive as soon as possible. With the increase in following came the increased revenue opportunity. The increased revenue began to slow our cashburn and quickly helped us reach profitability.

What is important to note is that these things started happening when our following was under 30,000 overall. We didn't need to be at 100,000 total social media followers in order to begin to see these benefits. But as we kept on growing, the frequency of these opportunities also increased.

Do you Need 100,000 followers?

I don't believe you NEED 100,000 followers in order to grow your business. "Massive" is a relative term. Like I mentioned earlier, we started seeing benefits much earlier than our 100,000 total and continue to see benefits as we are closing in on the 250,000 follower mark. But you DO NEED FOLLOWERS. Without followers who care about what you have to say, your influence is limited. And your competition, who has access to your customers, may get the leg up on you.

Sure, you don't necessarily need 100,000 followers or even 50,000. But why not reach that high? Why not try to reach, influence, and touch as many people as possible? If you believe that you have something of value to offer to this world, why not offer it? If you have thoughts, opinions, a mission, or a cause that you are passionate about, why not create your own community of people that want to hear what you have to say?

As a team, StartUp Mindset holds certain values. You can see those values in the articles we write. So even though we are a part of a business, we use the platform to help spread those values to our followers. You can do the same.

This book will help you do that.

CHAPTER 2
THE LANGUAGE OF SOCIAL MEDIA

"The limits of my language means the limits of my world."

-Ludwig Wittgenstein

Social media was not designed to be something used to generate money for businesses. This is the primary reason why so many entrepreneurs have trouble utilizing social media to grow their business. We entrepreneurs are used to investing time, money, and energy into something and then evaluating the return on investment. Facebook, Instagram, Snapchat, and Twitter were all designed as social tools. When was the last time you evaluated ROI on the time you spent with your family?

Since these platforms are not at their core business tools, businesses need to speak the language of the platform before seeking to sell something. It is the language of social media.

When Twitter started, there was an explainer video to show so that visitors would know what they were supposed to be doing when they joined. Twitter was originally designed to be a place where your friends and family could get updates on what you've been up to. Since blogging had already been around for a number of years before Twitter arrived, they called these short updates "microblogging."

What the platform evolved into was a way to voice not only what you were up to, but what you were thinking and feeling. Facebook, at the time, did not have a feature that allowed you to update your friends, but they soon found value in the idea and added their own news feed.

- 25% new posts about you, your thoughts, what you feel is important.

- 25% sharing posts, blogs, websites, and similar things that are not yours but are relevant to your audience.

- 40% interacting with other people, engaging in conversations on important, relevant topics.

- 10% advertising products you love, your own brand, self-promotional content.

The Languages of Social Media-Recreating Human Interaction

A secret to successful social media connecting is having the ability to engage in human interactions while limiting the cumbersome aspects of those interactions.

We've identified five major "languages" that are spoken on social media. These languages are how users of the medium speak to each other. These languages spark emotions and build relationships. These languages also encourage engagement and drive sales.

The five major languages are connection, being heard, entertainment, influence, and sharing. Most of what people are doing on social media stem from these five languages. Even though there are hundreds of other reasons why people use social media, we are going to look at only these five.

Connection

The obvious initial intention of social media was connection. The first real recognizable social networking platform, SixDegrees.com, was launched in 1997. The site was named after the six degrees of separation concept and allowed users to list friends, family members, and acquaintances both on the site and externally. Sixdegrees was able to attract 3.5 million users before it was sold in 1999 for $125 million.

This opened the door for more social networks such as Myspace and Linkedin to gain a foothold on the market. Since then, there have been several prominent social media sites that have emerged and countless other failed platforms that attempted to capture the desire of human being to connect with one another.

One of the reasons why Facebook was able to rise to the level at which it currently sits was its ability to allow users to stay connected with people without requiring them to directly speaking to each other. It was a perfect mix of staying in touch with the actual "touching." At the same time, Facebook mimicked human connection by creating the ability to form groups, communicate publicly and privately, and being able to share their life with the people they care about.

If you or your business can connect with people on social media in a very human way, you will have an advantage over those who are misusing the medium. As we mentioned before, one of the secrets to successful social media connection is to engage with humans online the way that humans connect offline; but better.

Being Heard

"Being heard is so close to being loved that for the average person, they are almost indistinguishable." - David Augsburger

The next social media language that is important to understand is also a human desire that we all have. Couples want their partners to hear them. Teenagers want to be heard by their parents. And your customers want to know that when they speak, they will be heard. And social media is one of the best ways to do that.

It is true that being heard often feels like being loved, valued, respected, and cared for. It is almost unbelievable to imagine that those basic human needs can be transmitted over a wifi connection. But they are, and those feelings are being met millions of times per day on social media.

Being heard is also important to humans because of our desire to be appreciated. According to the Department of Labor, lack of appreciation is the number-one reason people quit their jobs. Yet, according to a survey conducted last year by the John Templeton Foundation, only 10% of adults say thanks to a colleague every day, and just 7% express gratitude daily to a boss.

On social media, your followers want to feel like you appreciate them. They want to know that if they interact with you that you will be responsive. They want to feel a certain level of respect, love, and value from you.

Letting your followers know that you will be there to listen when they have questions or concerns about your business shows them that you will listen and be attentive when they actually do business with you. How you handle email communications, incoming phone calls, and yes, social media interactions gives your clients the image of what to expect from you. So use your time wisely and listen well.

Entertainment

On the other end of the spectrum of finding meaning and validation in life is the desire to be entertained. Even though we entrepreneurs want to deliver value, insight, and information, most of the people who are on social media are not necessarily looking for those things the majority of the time.

According to Global Web Index (GWI), 60% of people want to be entertained by social media content, more than any other reasoning for consuming content. The GWI's showcase reported that 6 in 10 social networkers use social media seeking entertainment. This is why of the top 10 most followed Twitter accounts, eight of the accounts are either athletes, actors, or musicians. The other two are former President Barack Obama and the official account of YouTube.

Because of the need for entertainment by the masses, does this mean that you need to continue to post videos of kittens and memes in order to have high engagement? Absolutely not. When users of social media visit these platforms, they do so looking for content they enjoy. Not necessarily content that makes them laugh or that they can sing along to.

The key for you and your business is to create and post content that people will enjoy. Later in this chapter, we will give you some ways to do just that.

Influence

Influence on social media is a hard thing to define. It is commonly thought that influence is how many followers you have and how many people you reach. But that is not at all what influence is. **Influence is how many people you move.** What good is it to have a ton of followers if you cannot influence them to take action?

Depending on how influential you are, a single post can drive sales, cause uproar, or even cause valuations to plummet. In February 2018, reality TV star Kylie Jenner sent a single tweet that shows how influence works.

Kylie Jenner
@KylieJenner

Follow

sooo does anyone else not open Snapchat anymore? Or is it just me... ugh this is so sad.

1:50 PM - 21 Feb 2018

75,832 Retweets **376,672** Likes

5.2K   76K   377K

This seemingly innocent post caused Snapchat's stock to drop 6 percent — an estimated loss of around $1.3 billion in market value. There are several other factors that may have contributed to Snapchat's market value trending downwards, but it is clear that Jenner's Tweet dealt a major blow.

Having influence just means that people trust what you post and that you have a certain level of authority. Even though Jenner is in no way connected to Wall Street and is not a tech expert, she is a powerful user of Snapchat's product. She also has millions of people who emulate what she does.

You and your business need to build the ability to move the people in the same fashion. **You want to be able to publish a post for a new product and discount and have those who see it take action.** You must develop the kind of reliability and clout that causes your followers to take anything you say seriously.

Part of this is developing an exceptional product and service. The other part is building credibility with your target audience.

Sharing

One of the last languages that is important to understand is the language of sharing. Not only is sharing on social media a language, it is also the currency. Nothing happens on social media without sharing. But sharing is not the same thing as posting. Sharing is a skill or even an art.

This is the language that we spoke which helped us grow. During the early days of our existence, we used social media to share any and everything that was valuable. It didn't matter if we created it or not. In fact, for months we primarily only shared information, resources, images, and videos from other platforms.

This didn't drive traffic or revenue to our site, but it did give us great insight into what people were interested in. Interesting enough, it was the same thing that interested us. We used that understanding to continue to build our audience and our reach.

Buzzfeed Chief Revenue Officer Andy Wiedlin says this in relation to sharing on social media "People share things that make them look clever and cool. They are building their own personal brands," Wiedlin said. "We spend a lot less time thinking how to target and a lot more thinking what people are sharing."

When sharing on social media, there are a few questions you have to ask yourself. Did this make me laugh? Did I learn something from this? Did I say wow? Would I email this to someone? Did someone ask about this? Did this make me smile, make me happy, etc?

In order to be effective on social media, you must be able to speak one of these languages fluently. There is no way around it! You must also be able to converse in at least one other language if you want to stay relevant.

How to Speak the Language

Treat Each Platform Like an Individual Person

Just like in real world communication, in order to speak to someone, it is important to know what language they speak. If you were to travel to a foreign country, you would need to know the language and customs of people of that country. The same is true for speaking the language of social media.

First seek to understand before you are understood. Learn how the people of the platform communicate with each other. For example, on Facebook choosing a number of the many emoji reactions is much more common and expected. While on Twitter emoji responses are good, but the most flattering form of approval is retweeting with a mention.

Posting to Instagram 10 times a day can come off as spammy to many users. But on Twitter, more frequent posting can help grow your following if what you are sharing is insightful, valuable, and genuine. Pay close attention to the way the platform is being used before you develop and execute your strategy. Later in this book, we will give you more insight into the language of each platform so that you will have a head start in understanding how each platform "speaks."

Start Listening Closely

Since being heard is one of the major languages of social media, one of the best ways to stand out and grow your influence is to make others feel as though they have been heard. When people feel as though you value their opinion, you connect with them in a deeper and more meaningful way. People are more likely to listen to you as well if they feel as though you are willing to listen to them.

This is not only true when it comes to social media, but also in the real world as well. A study published online in the *Journal of Experimental Social Psychology*, supports the idea that for the disempowered group, the biggest barrier to reconciliation is the belief that their concerns are being ignored. In other words, **when individuals were given a chance to share their stories and experiences with people from the other side, it helped improve their attitude about the "opposing group."**

This study was conducted using individuals who attended "peace camps." To help promote peace in the Middle East, many organizations have established "peace camps" or similar conflict-resolution programs that bring Israelis and Palestinians together to foster greater understanding of the opposing group. This MIT study found that there were greater benefits to those members in the less empowered groups.

"If that sense of being neglected and disregarded and taken advantage of is the biggest obstacle to progress, from their perspective, then you can partly address that by providing an experience of being heard," says Saxe, an associate professor of brain and cognitive sciences and associate member of the McGovern Institute for Brain Research at MIT.

The researchers found the same phenomenon in a similar study of Mexican immigrants and white Arizonans.

The people who make up your target audience want to be heard. They have problems that perhaps you can fix. Perhaps you can fix their problem via a product or service. Maybe you can't. In either case, make sure you listen and respond to them.

Here are some ways to make sure that your followers are being heard:

Respond and Retweet-Your social media feed should be active with interactions with the people who follow you. On our Twitter account, we often retweet many of our follower's content. Especially if they share one of our articles.

When your audience speaks either to you or someone else, let them know that you were listening. Let them know that you understand. Give your insight, praise, and respect.

Random Shout Out-Most brands like to announce an accomplishment by thanking their followers when they've reached a certain milestone, i.e., 10,000 followers or subscribers. Although this is a well meaning gesture, the accomplishment is more about the brand and not those who follow it.

Instead, take time to say thank you for their awesomeness without you being involved. It is also important to give random shoutouts to those individuals who interact with you the most or contribute to your community.

Be a Comment Ninja-Liking a post is easy and can be a great way to engage. The same can be said about using emojis. However, nothing is better than using your words. Every social media platform allows users to leave comments on content.

If you want to fulfill your customer's desire of being heard, use your words and leave thoughtful, insightful comments. This is also a good strategy for engaging with people of influence in order to get their attention.

Build trust; maintain trust

To speak the language of influence, you must learn to build trust and remain trustworthy. Having an audience that trust your thoughts, opinions, and recommendations is crucial for turning your followers into customers.

So how do you build trust on social media? The same way you build trust offline; be true to yourself and others. When you post on social media, you are creating an image of who you are and what you think. Sharing information that is valuable and trustworthy is key to building trust.

You must not also trick or mislead people into following you. Starting a social media relationship under misleading pretenses will make it easier for your followers to unfollow you. It will also make it harder for you to turn those followers into customers if they have to think twice about whether or not they trust you.

Here are some of the ways to build trust:

Be transparent-Be open and honest about your business and its operations. Obviously you do not want to share everything about your business, such as financial data or internal policies. But you do want to be transparent about who you are, what you do, and what you stand for.

Be Accountable-You must be accountable for your actions on and offline. If your business receives negative press or if your latest product was not up to par, you must be able to own your missteps and correct them. Running and hiding just makes you look like you're not willing to admit that you made a mistake.

Be Authentic-Your brand needs to be clear about your intentions. Why are you on Twitter? Are you there to spam and self-promote? Or are you there to connect, share, and answer questions. If you are there to connect but you never like, retweet, or talk with anyone, you just made yourself a liar. The user of these platforms can smell out a person or brand that is there with ulterior motives.

Show emotion

Earlier, we told you that in order to succeed on social media you must be able to connect in a human way. One of the things we humans are notorious for is having emotions. These emotions can power us to create change or they can break up down and break us apart. These same emotions can cause us to share in good things and be angry at bad things.

Showing emotion on social media means that you care about things other than yourself. It means that when something important to you and your business happens that you respond to it accordingly. It is absolutely possible to do this without getting into politics or highly controversial societal issues. It just means that you show an array of emotional reactions

Has a pioneer in your industry recently passed? Show respect and send your condolences through social media. Has a person in your sector reached a new level of accomplishment. Congratulate them publicly and celebrate with them. Is there something funny in pop culture that is happening that relates to your business? Poke fun at it and yourself by posting a meme.

Show your followers your serious side, your humorous side, your contemplative side, as well as your professional side. Try to balance how you do this in order to not muddy up your message or mission. Be sure not to overdo it.

Make them better

Robert Baden-Powell was the first to be credited with the quote "Leave this world better than you found it."

That should be one of your aims when it comes to the people who consume your social media content. It is possible to inform and promote your business in a way that people enjoy.

I was once having a conversation with a guy who had left his job to become a real estate agent. When he found out what I did and my experience in social media, he asked me how he could find highly motivated and qualified buyers online.

After digging into his business model a little more and finding out that he wanted to target first time home buyers, I told him to begin posting videos on the home buying process. I suggested that he publish short and long videos answering some common questions. I also suggested that he create a long 30 minute video.

He mentioned to me that he didn't like that idea because he didn't want to "give away everything." I told him that he won't give away everything and that if he could answer every possible question a person buying a home might have in a 30 minute video, he should be doing more with that skill than just selling homes.

When marketing on social media, people do not want to feel misled or that their intelligence was insulted by a promotion that seems spamming. They also don't want to watch or read information that is just a leadup to a sales pitch. Your audience will feel better about you and your brand if they feel good after consuming your content.

Use video
We will talk more about using video later in this book, but you should be beginning to think about using video

in your social media marketing as soon as you can. As we mentioned earlier, the only non-human account that ranks in the top 10 followers on Twitter is YouTube, a website that deals exclusively with video. That is not a coincidence.

For the majority of the population, watching a video is much more entertaining than reading. Use this to your advantage by using video in your media posts. Being witty and entertaining is often easier when done on video.

Publish "just for fun" post

Redbull energy drinks have a long history and the reputation of have some of the most entertaining social media feeds among big brands. Whether it is a skydiver, extreme skier, or a T-Rex riding a BMX bike, the brand consistently posts stuff that people want to watch. They also do a great job of tying that content back to their brand.

But just because your business has nothing to do with other exciting events doesn't mean you cannot publish the occasional "just for fun" post. These posts give your feed a little variety and fun.

Here are a few ideas for "just for fun" posts:

- *Random questions: "If I won the lottery, the first thing I would do is_____"?*

- *Behind the Scenes photos: Show the process not just the results.*

- *Relevant memes*

- *"Caption this" photo: Post a photo and ask your followers to come up with the perfect caption.*

- *Celebrate a little known holiday from another country.*

- *Post a "truth or fiction" question: Let your fans guess whether it's the truth or a myth.*

- *Hop on a trending topic or trending hashtag.*

You need to make sure that you are not taking yourself too seriously on social media.

Tell stories

Everyone will loves a good story, and everyone will listen to a storyteller. Telling great stories is a way to get your audience to listen to you. Instagram is the perfect place to do this. We will show you how to do this effectively in our Instagram chapter. The entire movie industry hinges on the ability to tell and retell stories that people want to pay attention to. This entire idea translates well to digital marketing.

Does your business have a good founding story? Is there a customer that you have impacted in a major way? Is there a member of your team that has a awesome and relevant tale to share. Consistently share stories that move people.

The stories you tell do not necessarily need to be your own. Begin to seek out interesting stories or events, and learn to craft those events and deliver them to your audience in an engaging way. Good stories consist of many elements including conflicts, heroes, and resolution. Be on the lookout for the stories you come across that contain those elements and start sharing them.

CHAPTER 3
GETTING READY TO REACH

"...because to influence a person is to give one's own soul."

-Oscar Wilde

Being on social media is the easy part, but using social media properly to further your business can be difficult. There are usually two paths which you can take: do it yourself or hire a third party agency.

Both require a social media marketing strategy to be in place before starting. For an agency, a marketing brief is usually preferred. This will allow them to understand a little bit about your company and what you want to be done.

Even if you do not wish to pursue an agency, creating a social media marketing brief is a good exercise. The easiest way to start is by asking yourself the following questions:

Who are you?
This covers the background of your organization. Provide detailed information on your company. This can cover anywhere from your businesses activities to your company history. Be sure to include your company's competitive advantages.

What makes your organization different from the competitors? In this section, you should also include a list of consumers, organizations, and other businesses your company intends to serve or work with. This will give the agency a full depiction of your business model.

After a brief company description, paint a picture of your organization's brand identity. Use personal attributes you would associate with your brand. Sometimes this is done by creating one-word adjectives that you feel describe your company.

For example, a computer company might use the words modern, electric, and fast to describe itself. Once you have a couple of words, expand these ideas into sentences. Another easy way to convey your brand identity is to <u>create a mission statement</u>. This should be a statement or sentence that describes your company's goals.

Following the brand identity, write about the vision of your company. This should be a mental image of where you want your business to be in the future. If you have the knowledge, include how you plan to achieve this vision. Showing your future steps to the agency can translate well into your social media marketing. It will allow the agency, or yourself, to create a better strategy around a clear vision.

Who is your audience?

This question should cover your target audience. Defining your target market can be difficult. Many businesses will say that everyone is within their target market, but this is simply not true.

Think of the group of people who will be receiving your product and/or service. This is the group of people you believe will want and use your product and service *the most*. Provide research to back up your claims.

After your target audience is defined, provide information on that demographic. This can include marital status, disposable income, or education levels.

Apart from demographic information, it is also important to show their behavioral patterns. How does this group of people interact with other businesses? Are they loyal? Does this group of people critique more than average? This is important for your social media. Understanding your target demographic and their behaviors can allow you to create better content that engages your audience.

Lastly, define your customer relationship. Describe how you want to interact with your audience around their behaviors. These can be principles, practices or even guidelines that your organization should follow when interacting with customers.

Specifically, for social media, this can include how you interact with an angry customer. Many people use social media as an outlet to review products and leave negative feedback on services. How will your company handle this?

What do you want to accomplish?

This will be the largest section in your social media marketing brief. This should cover your social media objectives and define your overall goal. Here are just a couple social media marketing objectives you can use:

Increase brand awareness. A study looked at key objectives and what senior marketers thought were important. 94% of respondents chose increasing brand awareness was a key objective. This marketing technique allows you to expose your product, service, and company to people in your target demographic. This may also include attracting new customers to drive online sales. A future goal would be to increase brand awareness outside your target demographic leading to more publicity.

- **Educate on brand updates and promotions-** This can be a tool for updating customers on important company information, including new product lines or company milestones. Promotions can include discounts or special offers that can increase customer traffic to your website.

- **Build up brand identity-**This can show your audience what defines your company. It may include advertising values that you find important or showing your company culture. This will allow customers to get a better idea about your entire company.

- **Feedback and support-**As stated above, social media can be used as an outlet for angry customers. An objective could be to analyze the feedback and to provide customer support. Interacting with customers is important and is one of many ways to successfully market your company.

- **Attract employees-**One way to utilize social media is to attract new employees. Showing a comfortable company work environment or simply posting job openings can increase the awareness of company opportunities.

After defining your objectives, the next step is to break down how these will be accomplished. Define the content that can be created specifically for each of the objectives you have named. An easy way to create a successful social media plan is to follow the SMART acronym. Be *Specific*, make sure the plan is *Measurable*, it should be *Accurate*, *Realistic*, and it can be done in a *Timely* manner.

For example, explaining the maintenance of your social media pages. This may include maintenance of media pages, content, design, photos, videos, etc. Another example is to define your brand voice that will be used to build brand identity.

Lastly, you must answer how will you measure the success of your objectives. This includes creating Key Performance Indicators (KPIs). These are measures that evaluate the success of the objective, usually quantifiable. For example, increasing brand awareness can have KPIs of new followers, a number of subscriber growth, average likes per post, etc.

Other Specifications

Although the previous question covers the majority of a social media marketing brief, it is important to have a couple other specifications. The first is IT specifications. You want to make sure your technical side is covered as you venture into new social media.

Next, define how you want to be presented with social media reports. If you are doing your marketing plan yourself, this may include searching for programs that give you reports. The data should be broken down easily and show the success of each social media campaign.

 Sprout Social is a great example of a social media reporting tool. If you are going to an agency, this is the part of the brief where you will state which ways you want to see your data. This includes the duration of reports (monthly, weekly, quarterly), format, and information.

Lastly, conclude with any additional information you deem important. This may include legal contracts between you and the agency such as intellectual property or a non-disclosure clause. Naturally, you want the brief to be tailored to your social media marketing needs.

How Much Should You Spend on Your Marketing?

Effective marketing strategies will increase your brand awareness and recognition and drive sales. While marketers have known that social media is an effective tool for years now, marketing budgets have shifted to reflect this.

Social Media Spending On the Rise

<u>A recent study from the Duke University Fuqua School of Business</u> found that social media spending is rapidly rising. They found that social media spending is roughly ten percent of overall marketing budgets. They anticipated that within five years, **marketers expect to spend more than 21% of their total budgets solely on social media marketing**.

This is a significant shift and has tangible consequences for businesses of all sizes. In general, marketing budgets are growing and more and more small businesses are finding themselves hiring dedicated marketers to develop and implement comprehensive strategies.
With this shift, more attention is being paid to budgeting for social media advertising, engagement, and analytics.

Obviously, your social media budget will be a component of your overall marketing budget. Determining the size of your marketing budget will depend on a number of qualities, such as the size of your business, how long the business has been operating, your needs, and the funds that are available for this purpose.

Keep in mind that cost can vary across different platforms as well. What you pay for Facebook advertising may be more cost effective, but perhaps your type of business will get a better ROI from promoted tweets.

Admittedly, these are very vague guidelines that rarely lead to any actionable advice. **Taking the idea that around 10% of a marketing budget is being spent on social media, you'll work backwards to determine the size of the overall budget.**

If You Are a New Business Prepare to Spend More

Young businesses tend to spend more on marketing than more established companies. That makes sense since in the early stages of operations you need to attract and grow a customer base, which requires a more comprehensive marketing strategy. In general, experts suggest that companies who have been in business for one to five years use between **12 and 20% of their gross revenue** (or projected revenue for the year) on marketing. Companies that are less than a year old should expect to spend more.

If that number seems scary or shocking to you, you aren't alone. It seems like an ironic twist that when your startup is in its infancy, you need to spend considerable amounts of money that you don't have to attract customers who will hopefully give you the money you need to attract more clients.

Marketing is there to help you carve out a new market share and to develop brand and product recognition with an audience who have no idea who you are. Once your brand has some recognition and you're able to maintain a customer base, you can start to parse down your marketing budget.

As with most things in life, you get out of marketing what you put into it. There are bare-bones approaches to marketing that are inexpensive, like hiring an unpaid intern, and there are more expensive and comprehensive plans, like hiring a corporate marketing agency.

Neither is necessarily better or worse, but different strategies will have varied impacts on your bottom line. The outcome of your social media marketing investment is your return on investment. While your ROI will ultimately be driven by revenue, you can also use different metrics like the number of new customers, increases in average sales, or unique visits to your social media pages.

Spend Where Your Customers Spend Their Time

When it comes to making your social media marketing profitable to your business, you want to focus your strategy and **invest your budget in the platforms that your customers are using**. It just doesn't make sense to spend a third of your social media budget on platforms like Twitter or Pinterest if the overwhelming majority of your customers use Facebook or Instagram instead. The key to a successful marketing campaign is to find out what drives your customers to purchase your product and to generate new leads.

For new startups that haven't fully established whether their target audience actually matches their consumer base, marketing will take on a more trial and error approach. Within your budget, you'll need to allocate for any losses incurred for strategies that don't generate their anticipated revenue.

Start with one or two online platforms and build your strategy from there. Facebook still dominates the social media scene, with over 1.7 billion active monthly users, though platforms like Instagram and Twitter have grown rapidly in recent years. Many startups choose to focus their early campaigns here by <u>sponsoring or promoting posts</u>.

You don't need to be on every single social media site, especially in the early stages where you don't have a dedicated social media marketer or the budget to hire an outside media strategist.

Rather, focus your attention on producing quality content that reaches your targeted demographic rather than looking to increase your follower count as quickly as possible. Remember, a high follower count isn't nearly as effective if those followers never actually purchase your products.

While keeping your social media marketing in-house offers you more control over the schedule and workflow, you may not have an employee who has the training or experience needed to <u>manage multiple social media pages</u> while producing effective content that engages with a broad client base.

At this point, you may need to hire an outside contractor or freelancer, though their rates can vary widely. As your marketing budget grows, hopefully in response to growing sales and revenue, you can designate funds for a social media expert.

Social media has been, and will continue to be, a major part of marketing. By all accounts, social media platforms are expected to continue to grow over the next few years, and your marketing budget should reflect this fact.

While bootstrapped startups will likely be unable to designate an employee to only work on social media marketing, the importance of a comprehensive marketing strategy can't be understated.

In this book, however, we **will not be spending a lot of time on the numerous paid options** available such as Facebook ads, Instagram ads, Youtube advertising and other options. Although some of our suggestions may require you to spend money, **the goal of this book is to help you build influence; not buy it.** Then to use that influence to grow your business's sales organically.

CHAPTER 4
GROW ON FACEBOOK

"How dare you settle for less when the world has made it so easy for you to be remarkable?"

-Seth Godin, sethgodin.com

Facebook was the first social media platform that StartUp Mindset used to get off the ground. It was also what helped me see if there was actually an audience for what I wanted the platform to be. During the early days, I watched very closely, what the fans liked and what they didn't.

It was very important for me to understand whether I had a viable business on my hands. The reason was because I planned on reaching out to other entrepreneurs and asking them to join in on the StartUp Mindset project. I really didn't want to do that unless I knew that people wanted what I had to offer.

One of pieces of advice I give to new entrepreneurs who have a product or business idea is to validate the idea with total strangers. When I started marketing our page, I did not invite any of my friends and family to like the page. I did this because I knew that they would probably like and share the content just out of support.

Although I always appreciate any support given, their engagement wouldn't have given me a clear idea of whether or not I was publishing quality content. I wanted to know that total strangers would like and follow a page just because they liked what they saw.

This made Facebook a valuable source of feedback for me, and helped shape the kind of content I would want to produce when the blog launched. Ultimately, I knew that I would only produce the type of content that was in line with the direction of the business. But Facebook helped me verify that I was attracting the type of followers that I wanted.

Facebook is almost unavoidable when it comes to sales potential. It least it should be for any business owner concerned with revenue growth. Even though new and established businesses alike are seeing the Instagram as a very effective alternative, Facebook is just too massive to ignore.

Personal Facebook Profile

Many people often just use their personal Facebook profile as a way to drive business. This is a good idea, since many of the people who are on your Facebook page already know you and (hopefully) like you. This also allows you to mention your business and business activities without it being spammy.

This is a huge advantage for entrepreneurs. Think about it. If you were to visit your Facebook feed right now and scrolled through, only paying attention to your friends posts and not content that they have shared, you would see that some of them will mention you and your business.

Facebook Page

A Facebook page is a public profile specifically created for businesses, brands, celebrities, causes, and other organizations. The major difference between profiles and pages is that pages do not gain "friends," but "likes" - which are people who choose to "like" a page. Pages can gain an unlimited number of fans, differing from personal profiles, which has had a 5,000 friend maximum put on it by Facebook.

Pages offer a way to update followers on events, promotions, and announcements that may interest your fans. If your business plans to engage in content marketing (which it absolutely should), then a Facebook Page will help get your content in front of more people.

Besides driving traffic to your Facebook page from outside sources such as other social profiles, your website, or email list, the only real way to grow your Facebook page in a sustainable way is by using Facebook ads and boosts. We will get into how to do that later in this chapter.

The problem with pages

In the past, a Facebook page was one of the best ways to engage, connect with, and sell to customers. Many businesses thrived with their ability to reach potential customers directly by posting deals and shareable content on Facebook that would appear in the news feed of their target market.

The key was to grow your likes in order to stay on the top of your followers minds. But slowly, Facebook started to change the game. Many pages started seeing their reach decrease as Facebook promoted other (non-free) options to reach people. We'll get into those options later but for now, you should know that many people were not happy.

But Facebook wasn't done. In early 2018, Facebook announced even more changes to their algorithm that had those publishing on Facebook pages very worried.

In an attempt to retain its emphasis on authenticity, Facebook announced that it would be demoting posts that ask for likes, comments, or tags to increase engagement.

The posts, coined "engagement bait" usually prompt the reader to "tag a friend that needs this!" or, "comment YES if you agree!" These posts are usually prioritized higher in the news feeds due to the amount of engagement they receive, although the content of the post may be low quality or "spammy."

In just the first move of an ongoing plan to continually improve and scale efforts to reduce engagement bait, individual posts from people and pages will be demoted. Within a few weeks, Facebook will continue their crackdown on a much broader scale to include the demotion of entire pages that repeatedly employ engagement bait to boost interactions.

Facebook has been taking steps in this direction for some time, making tweaks to amplify users' content while weeding out spam and clickbait.

As Facebook sends them less traffic, publishers have been diversifying away from Facebook and fishing for traffic on other platforms such as Google, Apple News, and Twitter

This does not mean that you should not have a Facebook page. It is important to reach people wherever you can find them. Facebook has the largest user base of any social media platform, which means that millions of people are only on Facebook. This means that Facebook may be the only way you reach your ideal client via social media.

Facebook Groups

A Facebook Group is a place for group communication and for people to share their common interests and express their opinion. They let people come together around a common cause, issue, or activity to organize, express objectives, discuss issues, post photos, and share related content.

You can share products, ask for help, and offer services

on many Facebook groups. Anybody can set up and manage their own Facebook Group, and you can even join up to 6,000 other Groups.

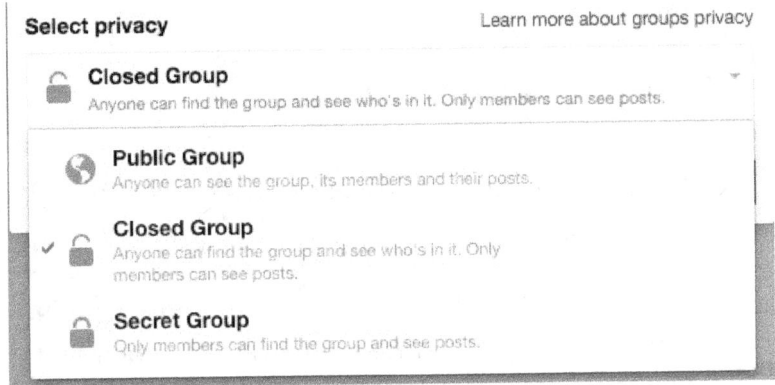

Closed Facebook Groups

When a group is closed, only those who have been invited to the group can see the content and information shared within it. The group itself appears in Facebook searches, and the description and member list are visible to anyone on Facebook.

Secret Facebook Groups

The only way to find and join a secret group is to be invited by an existing member. These groups offer a higher level of security and stealth. This group will not appear anywhere on your profile, and only those within the group can see who the members are and what is posted.

Public Facebook Groups

This is where you should start. Public Facebook groups are just that; public. All members' posts are fully visible to all other Facebook users. These groups usually contain the largest number of members, since there are no invitation requirements. These groups also have the potential to grow very quickly for the very same reason.

Using Groups to Grow Your Reach

The beautiful thing about Facebook groups is that it is not as hard as you think to stand out. Even with a group of 50,000, it is possible to gain visibility. The reason this is possible is due to the fact that most people are using groups the wrong way.

Most use groups to promote themselves without asking questions and offering answers.

Establish yourself

The key to making connections is to offer as much assistance as possible. When you join a group, it is a good idea to introduce yourself. Let everyone know who you are and what you do. From there, you must prove that you have something of value to add to the group.

Becoming a group celebrity

Once you've introduced yourself, it is time to prove yourself. Be sure to turn on your notifications for the groups where you want to be the most active. Facebook will send a notification to your phone when members of the group post questions and content.

When you see those notifications for recommendations, questions, or statements, try to be one of the first people to comment on the post. By doing this, you will be one of the first profiles that are seen when other people within that group check the comments for that post.

Also, the person who published the post will be more likely to engage with you, since you were one of the first to respond. If the post becomes populated with comments, those who are late to the conversation are usually ignored by the person who published the post. I mean, no one wants to answer 50 comments.

Using Boost to Grow a Following

To make this easy, we are going to show you some simple ways to grow your reach on Facebook.

Here is a 9 step plan that we used to grow our Facebook following by the 1,000's in 14 days.

Step 1-Test Content

Once you get your hands on over 100 genuine followers, begin testing different types of content. Throw in a mix of content from your website/blog, some content from other reliable sources in your niche, images, and video. You can also post some motivational images.

Do this daily for at least seven days. Once you've completed the posts, take a look at your Facebook page analytics. See which posts performed the best. In particular, notice the posts that have the most shares.

Step 2- Write an awesome article or find one.

Next you need to find a piece of content that you will use to draw in more people. The content could be one of your own or one from an outside platform. If you are looking to drive traffic to your blog or website, create an article and publish it on your blog. If you just want to draw attention to your page, you can use someone else's link.

Make sure that the article is quality and highly shareable. You should be able to decipher what kind of content your audience will respond to by looking at the data from the previous week's test.

If you don't mind if the link goes to another site, all you need to do is find an article or video from another site that you know will be shared often. This does not mean that you steal someone else's content and publish it on your blog or website. Most publishers (StartUp Mindset included) run plagiarism tests every so often to see if any sites have republished their content without permission. You don't want to get into trouble, but you can share the link on your Facebook page.

If you are in the startup, B2B, or entrepreneurship space and are having a hard time finding an article of someone else's to publish, fee free to use one of ours.

Here are a few that have performed well on StartUp Mindset's Facebook page.

-10 billion dollar companies that started as home businesses
link: https://startupmindset.com/10-billion-dollar-companies-that-started-as-home-businesses/

-10 Ultra Successful Entrepreneurs You Didn't Know Were Introverts
https://startupmindset.com/10-successful-introverted-entrepreneurs/

-Generation Z is About to Enter the Workforce. Here's What You Need to Understand About Them
http://startupmindset.com/generation-z-is-going-to-change-the-game-heres-what-you-need-to-understand-about-them/

Step 3-Make sure your feed looks great

Once you've got your content, review your feed once again. Take a look to make sure there is other attractive content. In the coming steps, you've going to drive a lot of people to your page, but there are several things that will determine if they follow you or not. Think of the old saying "you can lead a horse to water but you can't make hime drink." We'll see that you can drive a customer to your page but you can't make them like.

You can, however, entice someone to like your page by having a great looking feed. Make sure to mix up the content and to remove any published posts that have not performed well or posts that your current followers plain hate.

Here are some things people look for right before they like:

- Profile image and Banner
- Who you are
- Your audience size

- What you're publishing
- How often you're posting

Step 4- Publish the Awesome Post

Now you're reading to publish the post you've discovered will be shared by some of your followers. Go ahead and place the content and click publish.

If you were right in knowing your audience, you should see a few likes and maybe a few shares. Observe the post for the next 24-48 hours to see how many shares it receives and how much engagement it gets. Also check to see how many of the people who've seen the post clicked the link.

Step 5-Boost Post

When you publish a post on Facebook, you have the option of boosting the post in order to give it more visibility. Depending on your budget, you have the option of reaching people who like your page or a completely new demographic. If you already have a following (I'd say 500 or more) I suggest you boost the post to those individuals and their friends. There is a very good reason why this should be done.

By showing the post to people who already like your page you are engaging with people who already know who you are and like your stuff. So when you boost a post to reach them, you increase the chances of engagement and social shares.

If you have set aside a budget for your Facebook following, I would use it here. To start, set the boost for the post to $100. Set the campaign anywhere from 14 to 30 days. You have to be sure that the image used for the post does not contain a lot of text. Facebook hates this and your boost will not be accepted.

Step 6- Watch the engagement happen

Once you set your boost, you will see a lot of engagement. You will see likes, loves, laughs, and shares. If you are not seeing a lot of engagement once your reach is in the 1,000s, edit the posts text to see if you can start a dialog. Say something interesting, funny, or ask a question. This will usually increase and encourage engagement. Once again, be sure **not** to ask the audience to share or to like. Facebook can penalize the post or page, and label it spammy

Step 7-Invite Strangers to Like

Now, here is your opportunity to find new people to engage with. **Click on the engagement icons** on the post. There you will see all of the individuals and pages that liked the post. To the right of those profile icons, you will see a button.

The button will either say "Like", "Liked" or "Invite." If the button reads "like," this means that the profile that engaged with the post is a Facebook page. If it reads "liked," this means that the page or person has already

liked your page. If it reads "Invite," this means that the profile has not yet liked your page.

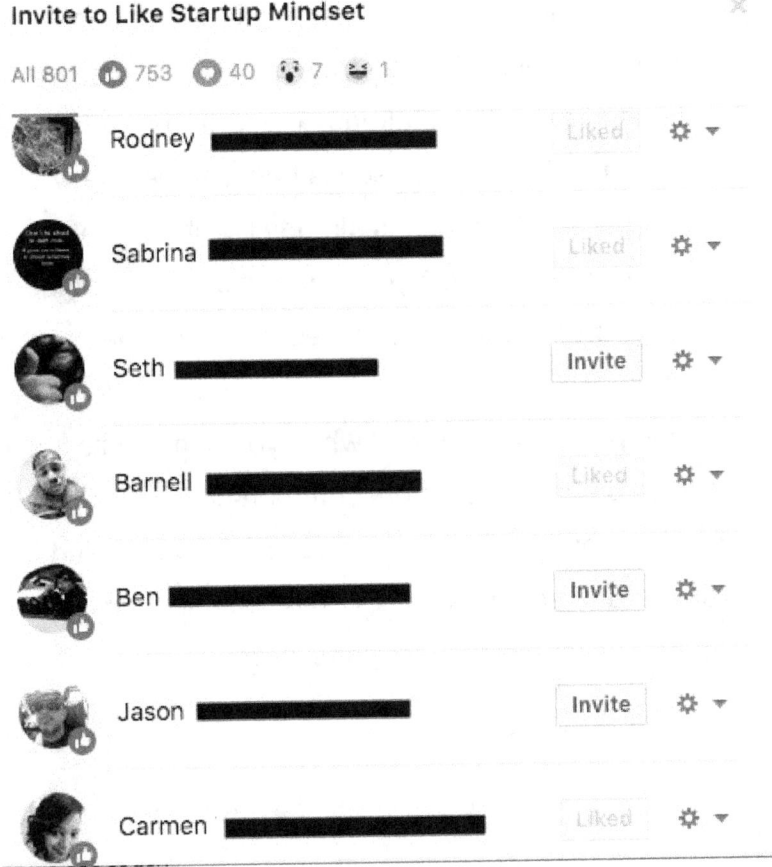

This is when you strike, click invite on the profiles that you would like to send an invite to like your page. Hopefully, those who are invited to like the page are friends of people who already like your page. The reason this is an advantage is because people will likely like a page if their friends already like it. When you invite someone to like your page, they will see that one of their friends already vouches for your page.

It is important to note that when you send invites, you will be sending them from your personal Facebook profile, not your business page. If you don't mind being the face of your business, continue to send invites to everyone who liked your page.

Step 8-Pin Post to Top of Your Facebook Page

Once your boost is over, you can still use this post to acquire new followers without spending money. You can do this by pinning the post to the top of your Facebook feed. Pinning the post means that when someone visits your page, this post will be the first they see.

If you are still driving people to your Facebook page by placing a Facebook icon on your website, email signature, and other means, you will see that this post will continue to spread on its own. It may be at the rate of when you originally boosted it, but it should continue to get likes and shares.

Step 9-Continue inviting

Over the next few months, you can continue to use this technique to promote other posts that you feel will gain some traction. Or, if you want to use your social media budget for Facebook ads or on other platforms, you can revisit the pinned posts occasionally to see if there are any new profiles that reacted to the content.

CHAPTER 5
GROWING ON INSTAGRAM

"Find your sweet spot: the intersection between what you know and what your customers need to know."

-Joe Pulizzi

Instagram has turned into a goldmine for those who want to launch and promote their personal or professional brand. There are countless stories of million-dollar businesses that never would have existed if it weren't for Instagram. There are also a plethora of influencers who have created sustainable lifestyle businesses by promoting the products they love.

Instagram is unique in that no other social media platform has enabled the kind of sales results for new businesses without needing to use the platform's built-in advertising options.

On StartUp Mindset, we've interviewed several entrepreneurs, influencers, and bloggers who have reaped rewards of having influence on Instagram. One blogger we've interviewed is Paola Alberdi. Paola's Instagram following currently sits at 765,000. Her blog is called Blank Itinerary which is an online website mostly about fashion, lifestyle, home decor, travel and more. Her entire business started off as sharing photos on Instagram of her travels when she got married and went to amazing places on my honeymoon.

Right before getting married, she quit her job where she worked as brand manager for three products because the company was moving to Mexico and she didn't want to move. Paola has always loved fashion so after returning from her honeymoon and trying to figure out what to do with her life, she thought she'd give blogging a try. Four years later, she is running her blog full-time and has no plans to return to working a corporate job.

During the interview, we asked Paola to share her philosophy on creating content on Instagram. Her response echoes what we have presented earlier about the importance of connecting in a very human way.
"I like to create content that people can relate to and aspire to.", Alberdi says. "People tell me that they feel like they are my friends even though we have never met and that is the most incredible feeling. Of course, as bloggers, we have learned how to create aesthetically appealing photos, but there are different styles of fashion bloggers and the vibe of the content can be very different. I feel like most of my content is usually natural, real and in the moment".

She also subscribes to the idea that influence and growth takes time and consistency. When trying to grow your reach, speed is not the most important thing; quality is. "I feel like everyone wants immediate results but it takes a lot of work and time. You need to have patience and be consistent. You need to invest the time to create unique and amazing content. I would also say, to stay authentic. Don't try to be exactly like everyone else because the things that make you different is what will attract people".

Another upcoming interview that will be posted on StartUp Mindset is of Hismile founders Nik Mirkovic and Alex Tomic. Hismile sells teeth whitening kits that work within 10 minutes. The two founders were barely out of their teens when they started the company.

Their entire company started on Instagram. By using the power of Instagram influencers, they have been able to grow their following to over 750,000 followers. This translated into business success as they went from **$0 to $50 million in sales in just under 3 years!**

StartUp Mindset has also seen benefits of utilizing this platform. We didn't officially launch our Instagram page until late 2017. But we have been able to attract thousands of followers in just under a 3 months. It amazed us how we could increase traffic by just posting a few times per week. Users on Instagram tend to engage more than Facebook in our experience.

Getting Going With Instagram

Instagram grows at a rate of **nearly 500,000 new users a day**. Those users are active as well; Instagram users like an average of 4.2 billion posts every day. So how does your startup get in on some of those likes and increase your app engagement?

As an inherently visual platform, Instagram attracts brands that have products which translate well in visual representations. You're more likely to find a fitness brand selling athletic wear or exercise products on the app than a consulting management firm. While it's not my place to tell you whether you can (or should) use Instagram, it's wise to consider whether your brand will translate well in this visual medium.

A social media presence has become a necessary, rather than a potential, part of marketing your startup.

Since there is a low cost to entry (the Instagram app is free), anyone can become a part of this platform.

While you'll pay to sponsor your posts, advertising on Instagram is an effective way to engage with your customers, expand your customer base, and to sell your product. There have been over 40 billion photos shared to date, and there are an average of 95 million photos and videos shared every day. Standing out among those kind of numbers is difficult, but not impossible.

Post Frequently

On Instagram, users have feeds that continually update as the profiles they follow post new content. As you post new photos and videos, they will appear as active viewers refresh their feed. A 2016 study conducted by Forrester found that the **top 50 global brands post content on average of 4.9 times per week**. This is more than double the 2015 average, and reflects an increase in engagement and user demand for new content. However, do not sacrifice quality for the sake of quantity. One well-executed post that draws significant engagement will drive your revenue returns more than three poorly executed posts.

Maintain a Visual Identity

Just as with any other branded image, you need consistency across platforms. Filters are frequently used on Instagram, and can boost the appeal of your images to your viewers. Creating and maintaining your signature branded look on Instagram links your content to your brand identity.

Pick a filter and stay with it. This way, users will see continuity across images when they are on your profile's landing page. The types of images that you use on your profile should reflect your brand's personality, identity, and echo the type of relationship you want to have with your followers and consumers.

A startup in the beauty industry may want to portray an image of sophistication as an iconic and classic style. The photos and videos that you would post on your feed would use captions and images that reflect your unique brand identity. Any disconnect between your visual content and your brand, such as a fitness brand posting pictures of fried and greasy foods, risk coming off as inauthentic and insincere to users.

Follow Selectively

When you look at the profiles of major brands, you'll see that their follower to following ratio is high. This means that while they have high follower counts, they typically follow a much smaller percentage of users. As a public profile, users can see who your profile is following. While in the early stages of building up your follower count, you will likely need to follow a larger number of profiles to elicit in kind follows, it's wise to selectively follow users at later stages.

For instance, once you have a robust and engaged follower count, it'd be unwise to go on following sprees and follow other users at random. The people that you follow should be a reflection of your brand, and the image that you want to maintain. As a tech-based startup, it'd be wise to follow influencers in the tech world, other startups you have relationships with, and media personalities who write about technology.

Look Globally

80% of Instagram users are from outside of the United States. This can translate to huge global sales and the potential to expand your brand into previously untapped markets across the world. Engaging with a global audience may seem difficult at first, but can have major returns. Consider using hashtags in other languages to put your profile in non-English speakers' feeds, and posting content that appeals to international audiences.

Use Ads to Sell Not to Grow.

It may be tempting to throw money at Instagram advertising in order to grow your audience but we don't recommend it. If you choose to use Instagram ads, I highly suggest you use it for sales not branding. Using the advertising option is the only way (outside of Stories) where you can link directly to an outside website on an Instagram post.

This means that when you use the ads, you can link directly to a sales page. As of the writing of this book, Instagram only allows links back to your site in the bio of your Insta profile. Also note that you can link outside using Instagram Stories IF you have a following of over 10,000. This is another incentive to grow your following as fast a possible.

50% of Instagram users follow at least one business. Users are engaged with the businesses that they shop at, identify with, and are willing to purchase new products from. Advertising using your Instagram profile is easy. You can use a business profile, which allows you to add your website directly to your profile.

When you are ready to sell and know your target market, this is where I suggest you spend your advertising dollars on Instagram. According to Locowise, 75% of users take action, such as visiting a website link or purchasing a product, after they look at an advertising post.

Add Relevant Hashtags

Hashtags, such as those used on Facebook and Twitter, are used to connect users to posts and content that are relevant to their searches. When someone searches for "shoes" on Instagram, they are shown results from other users that use the hashtag, along with users who post content about the subject.

Research by Simply Measured has shown that posts that include at least one hashtag have 12.6% more engagement on average.

Using relevant hashtags with your posts is an easy way to increase your engagement, but will only drive your Return on Investment (ROI) when they are relevant. Simply, if you're using #shoes on a post that advertises your telecomm product, you're unlikely to drive any revenue.

How to Create an Exceptional Brand Aesthetic on Instagram

Instagram has over 500 million active users, and at least 30% of them purchased a product they had first seen on Instagram. What does it mean for your brand? It means you should swear by the platform.

It's no secret that social media users engage with visual content more than any other, and that's why developing a strong Instagram presence is a must for every brand that not only wants to sell but has an engaging story to tell.

According to Sprout Social, 70.7% of US businesses are using Instagram. But how many of them are doing it right? Posting randomly isn't going to work. Instagram is unapologetic when it comes to clumsy photos. So, to please the social media giant, let's learn some aesthetics.

Your Identity

Before getting creative with photos, you should be firm on what type of content you want to grace your feed. Your visual identity should be in sync with what your brand stands for. To develop a strong and genuine connection with your followers, let them know what the story of your brand and its core values are. Let's say, if you are proud of your company culture, take a couple of snaps to show it!

Instagram is actually full of appealing images. But what's the point if it's so difficult to tell them apart? The point isn't having pretty photos, but making someone instantly recognize your brand. So make sure that every photo you post is a reflection of your brand's identity.

Your Target Market

You've got your identity now, but social media channels are a two-way street. If you want users to act, you should know exactly whom you are targeting. Your followers are your potential customers, so find ways to bring them into the conversation.

The best way to appeal to your target market is to learn from them. Look at what type of content your followers and customers are sharing. Really, there is no better way.

Another way is to integrate user-generated content into your feed, content that will complement your own aesthetic. For example, Airbnb has found a way to keep the balance between their aesthetic and user-generated content. In a sense, user-generated content has become their aesthetic. Sharing photos and stories from all around the world gives their feed a look that's

airbnb

1,848 posts   **3m** followers   **1,493** following

Airbnb Airbnb opens the door to interesting homes and experiences, even if it's just for a night. Share your stories with #Airbnb. Book from our feed: abnb.co/instagram

inspiring and impersonal. So look up to your followers, they can be creative too!

Instagram @Airbnb

Visual Consistency

Now we're getting into the nuts and bolts of brand aesthetic on Instagram. Consistency can be created mainly by sticking to one color scheme and subject matter.

Filter Use

Many people believe that the easiest way to a consistent aesthetic is by using the same filter. Actually, it's more complicated than it sounds, because other factors such as lighting play a role. So if you master all the aspects below, using the same filter would actually come in handy!

Lighting

If most of your photos are shot in natural light, and only a couple were done indoors, the difference can be drastic. Therefore, using the same filter over them won't help much. So determine what type of lighting suits well the vibe of your brand and try to stay true to it.

Brightness and Contrast

You should also be consistent when it comes to brightness and contrast. Photos with more brightness and contrast usually do better on Instagram, but be careful not to overdo it.

Shooting Angle

A useful tip that is rarely mentioned: taking photos from a consistent angle can greatly enhance your aesthetic. Many popular accounts on Instagram only upload photos shot from above. While that's the mainstream stand, feel free to find your unique angle!

Color Palette

Do you want to achieve a dark moody look, or do you want your feed to radiate with colors? Of course, the decision shouldn't be random and has to be linked to the identity of your brand. Brighter colors have proven to be more attractive. In fact, photos with bright colors are 592% more likely to get likes than the darker ones. But if bright colors don't suit your mission, forget about the impressive number above.

Using one color palette might be monotonous. And that might not be something you are going for. You can accentuate different colors in your feed, but the important thing is to make the transition smooth. See how Pantone does that by posting in color blocks. From four rows of turquoise, they move to a section of pastel pink and then transition to intense orange and red.

Subject Matter

Consistency should also apply to your subject matter. Take Coffee 'N Clothes's Instagram page as an example. They are very clear on their content, and their slogan stylishly caffeinated is there to prove it.
Thousands of people hit the follow button because they know exactly what the page has to offer. And when their photo pops up on your feed, it's just hard not to tell them apart.

Take a look at this Instagram page that posts vibrant photos. Their bio says "Stylishly caffeinated," and every photo they post lives up to that belief.

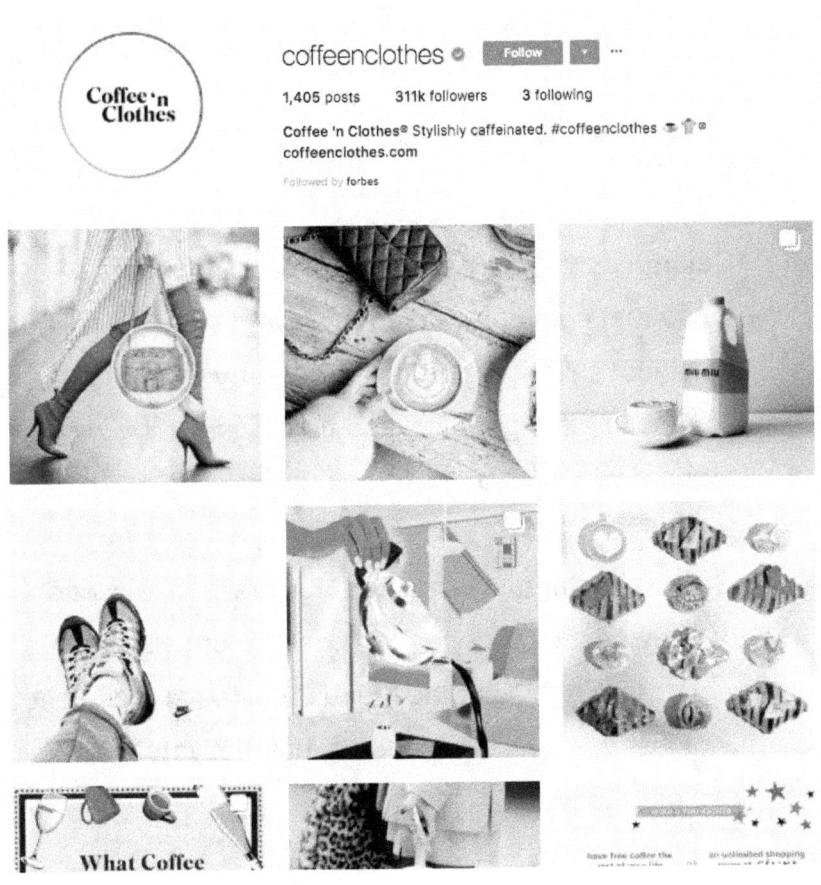

@coffeenclothes on Instagram

Now, your focus can be more diverse. Posting too much of the same thing risks being boring. However, too much diversity might leave your followers confused about the identity of your brand. And here is where balance comes into play. When playing around with different subjects and themes in your photos, try spacing them evenly across your feed. Don't cram them next to each other.

The Vibe

Colorful photos aren't enough. The best photos are those that communicate a narrative. In other words, don't just sell with your Instagram—try to establish a connection that goes beyond that. Think of building brand awareness as your main priority.

GoPro's Instagram is masterful in that sense. Not only do they post user-generated content, but also have a wanderlust feeling to their feed. Looking at those photos isn't just aesthetically pleasing, but motivates you to explore the world!

Planning

A killer aesthetic takes a lot of planning. Be prepared to shoot hundreds of photos, of which only ten will make it to your feed. You can use free apps such as Preview or UNUM to plan your Instagram feed.

Upload your photos, move them around, and see what looks best. And be prepared to kill your darlings. There will be individual photos that you will totally adore, but as soon as you put them in the feed, they'll lose their charm.

Creating a mesmerizing aesthetics is hard work, which requires great attention to details and intensive planning. While Instagram offers a lot of possibilities to promote your brand, it certainly isn't going to do the job for you. So make sure you know the rules, and think twice before sharing your photos!

Using Instagram Stories

By now you should be familiar with Instagram stories. Stories will work a little differently to your regularly pictures. These will only last for 24 hours, so if your followers miss them, they will disappear. That does also mean that they aren't added to your grid on your profile and this is one of the advantages – it's easier to post something a little more 'off message' here: perhaps something that is a bit of fun.

Each time you add a new photo, it will be added to your story and your fans will be able to watch those images and videos in a slideshow. Remember: your stories will appear at the top of the homefeed and will be indicated by a red ring circling your profile picture. Users who want to view your stories can then click on that image and will be able to sit back and watch the slide show, or swipe through images in order to speed it along.

Going Live

If you want to go live, then this will work just a little bit differently. All you need to do is open up the stories camera by swiping or clicking the plus button and then select the 'Live' option. This is found along the bottom next to the 'Normal' and 'Boomerang' options. A live tag will now appear on your Instagram Stories bubble, so that followers will know that they can tap it in order to see what you're doing live.

Your video will then disappear though, so make sure that you are careful to choose whether you would rather make a live video, a contribution to your story or a regular video upload! Something else neat about going live is that your followers will be notified even when they're not on Instagram (unless they have actively turned this off).

This increases engagement and it's a great way to get people to join in with whatever you're doing and to increase engagement and trust that way. At any time you can click to rotate the camera and if you select the 'Hands Free' option, then you'll be able to record without holding down the button.

This is useful for recording workouts or other things where you want to be in the shot and not talking to the selfie camera. During Your Live Videos During your live videos, you will notice comments appearing down the bottom if you are getting good engagement. These are the people who are watching your video right now and you'll also be able to reply to the comments.

But why reply to the comments by typing when you have the option to reply to the comments by voice? If someone asks a question, then just answer that question in person and while chatting. You'll also be able to see people appearing and disappearing in the live video and this is a good way to get more engagement – when you see someone join your chat, then why not welcome them and ask them how they are?

The first time you start watching a live video and this happens it feels very weird and it really shows the power of being live in a big way! Making Boomerangs You may notice that next to the Live option is another option called 'Boomerangs'. This is another new feature which is interesting and is essentially a very short, looping video. It works a lot like a GIF or perhaps the Live Photos from the iPhone.

Once in the Stories camera, simply click on the capture button and a burst of 10 photos will be taken automatically and stitched together into a 1 second video. This can then be played normally or in reverse. You can share these on Instagram, in your stories or even on Facebook and elsewhere. They look pretty cool and are certainly a good way to demonstrate tech savvy on your account.

Jump on the "Live" Bandwagon

Imagine how this could change our understanding of the world. Imagine if there was a natural disaster in a country where this had happened for instance. Forget news coverage: suddenly, the very best and most powerful way to learn about the disaster would be to tune in to all of the live footage being broadcast from friends, family, celebrities and strangers. It would be like virtual omnipresence – being able to see an event from countless different angles at once.

Live video essentially transports you to a place and time and it could change the way we consume news and media, the way we attend live events and more. And when this integrates with other future technologies – such as virtual reality and 360 cameras – then we can really expect to start transport ourselves to wherever our friends are and to experience events as though we were there.

And from a marketing standpoint, being able to talk directly to your fans is unprecedented. Think of your favorite celebrity. Think about someone you really admire. Now imagine if you knew they were going live and you could actually comment to them directly... they might even answer!

This is what you have the capability now to do – and your own fans will feel just as excited when you go live. While Stories might not have the same potential, these too have the ability to potentially alter the way we interact with our fans – to let us bring them with us on our travels and to grow the trust in that relationship.

This is crucial when it comes to selling. Someone is going to be much more likely to want to buy from you once they feel as though they know you – when they've seen just how your ideas and services have helped you in your own life and once they've seen you playing with your dog or celebrating Christmas with your family.

How to Create Great Stories and Live Videos

The first challenge when it comes to creating great stories, is to know which of your videos and photos are going to lend themselves best to your stories versus your main Instagram. Largely, the difference is whether you think of the photo as being quintessential to your brand and a great photo, or whether you think of it more as an aside – a little joke for the fans or a demonstration of something you've explained.

Likewise, more 'immediate' things work very well in your Stories, such as events. Let's say you have a fitness channel for instance and you're at a Bodybuilding competition chatting with people on stalls and meeting fans. Photos of the actual show will look great on your channel, as these demonstrate what your brand is about and can be made to look dramatic and spectacular.

A photo of you with fans though, or of you getting a sausage roll from one of the stalls will work much better in your stories. Meanwhile, video clips will work particularly well for the live video as they will give your audience a chance to attend along with you!

Always be sure to check copyright though before you go ahead and stream or you can risk getting yourself into trouble. If your brand does have a personal component, then as a rule, things that are your personal brand will work best for live or stories, whereas things that fit your corporate brand will work best on your grid as permanent additions.

Ask yourself: would you be happy for a photo to be a fan's first impression of your brand? If not, then it will work better as a story. The same goes for video, in which case you could share it live.

Content That is Great for Stories and Live

Certain content will of course lend itself particularly well to the Stories format or to being live.

Here are some suggestions:

Stories

- As mentioned, photos with fans are great for stories.

- Behind the scenes photos also work very well for stories and can be a great way to build anticipation for something. Got a new video in the works? Then why not post a photo of you filming or editing the video?

- Sequential photos – seeing as stories work like a slideshow, there are some fun effects you can pull off by uploading a few photos in a sequence. How about a few photos that show something you're cooking getting created?

- Photos that wouldn't be particularly attractive but that nevertheless fit your brand also work.

- You can also add photos that supplement the other photos you've taken. For instance, if you have taken 10 photos of the same activity, then you won't want to flood your account with them. Choose one or two for your grid and add the rest to your story.

- Stories are also a great place to shout out to another creator if you want to do a cross promotion!

- Jokes and funny asides also work great here!

Live Videos

- Travels – If you're traveling and you've come across something amazing, then why not let your followers come along with you for the ride?

- Events – The same goes for events. Bring your viewers to concerts, to premieres and to any other exciting events you might attend. In these cases, you can think of video as being a very natural extension to what you have previously been doing with your account – in this case, video will let your viewers almost experience that lifestyle you're promoting!

- Interviews – Let your visitors actually ask you questions and interact with you! Or how about conducting an interview with another personality and letting your viewers take part in that?

- Reviews and showcases – Got a product to promote? Why not showcase it live?

- Workouts

- Vlogs and discussions

CHAPTER 6
GROWING ON TWITTER

"Twitter is a great place to tell the world what you're thinking before you've had a chance to think about it."

-*Chris Pirillo, blogger*

Before Snapchat, the hardest social media platform to explain to your parents (and most people) was Twitter. The microblogging platform went from being a faster way to share updates to the best way to stay connected with just about anyone in the world.

Where else in the world can you read the spontaneous thoughts of the President of the United States and with a simple scroll, see which shades Kim Kardashian is wearing today? Nowhere but Twitter. This easy access to the lives and minds of many makes this one of the most addictive platforms for many people.

In the past, squabbles and bickering between two high profile individuals used to be reported by those who were there to witness them. Now, debates, disses, arguments, and spats are commonplace on Twitter.

But among all of the drama, there is an enormous amount of content being shared and business transactions taking place. There are some who still have issues understanding how to effectively use Twitter to grow their brand and business. In this chapter, we will breakdown how to use this conversation tool to grow your brand, business, and sales.

Basic Understanding of Twitter

Twitter is known as a micro-blogging site. Usually blogging consists of people setting up basic websites where they write about whatever they want. Micro-blogging, however, is different. What is unique about Twitter is that users are limited to posting messages of 280 characters or less. Posting a message is known as a tweet.

People make connections by following other people's twitter feeds. Once you click follow, anything that person or organization says will appear on your timeline. You can tweet a person by putting the @ symbol before their username.

Retweeting is also a big part of Twitter. This is where twitter users repeat tweets from other users to their own followers. This is one of the major ways of using Twitter.

A lot of activity on Twitter involves the use of hashtags. These are handles used to aggregate tweets about the same subject. For example, if a lot of people were attending a conference and wanted people to know what the speakers were saying, they would tweet to an agreed hashtag by using the # symbol followed by the agreed name.

News App or Social Media Platform?

Twitter is also the undisputed king of speed when it comes to the reporting of news. Twitter hastags spread like wildfire. Since sending a update via a tweet is fast and easy, and requires no images or video, many people will update much more frequently than on others platforms.

Before most media outlets report it, before the Wiki page changes it, and about a day before it begins trending on Facebook, thousands have probably Tweeted about it. When something is trending on Twitter, it is important. At least to many people.

Even though Twitter has found its sweet spot as the fastest news distribution platform on the planet, I also believe that it is the only true social media platform left. Twitter, to me, is the only online place (among the largest platforms) where conversations actually happen.

In chapter 1, we described to you how mimicking offline human interactions online is a secret to growing your following. When it comes to human conversation, no other platform does it better than Twitter.

You can connect with any leader, influencer, celebrity, athlete, CEO, or entertainer by just @replying them. Even if they have millions of followers, influential people check their mentions. They may not reply to them all or see every single one, but they absolutely see who is talking to them.

Sweet, sweet impressions

For years after going public, many people were claiming that Twitter was destined to become a dead platform. With Facebook blowing everyone out of the water, and Twitter's inability to sell itself to a larger corporation, many thought the social media platform would soon cease to exist.

But after years of speculation, Twitter surprised everyone with its profitability in 2018. The company attributed its improved finances to a focus on its strongest selling point: connecting advertisers and the people they want to sell things to in real-time.

"Twitter continues to help our partners be relevant in the moment at scale," chief executive Jack Dorsey said in the quarter's shareholders letter. Stronger ad sales in the crucial holiday quarter made up the difference for Twitter, even as the number of new people joining the site continued to stagnate.

There is nothing worse than publishing a post on social media, and Twitter offers advertisers and the rest of us something very sought after; eyeballs. We all want the opportunity to connect and sell to the masses. How can we do that if we cannot get in front of them?

Twitter and Instagram still allows users to share content that will actually be seen by those who follow them, compared to the consistent decline of the organic reach of Facebook pages As a business owner, you need to be able to take advantage of this opportunity.

For example, <u>at the Oscars this year,</u> Twitter generated 3.7 billion impressions on 24 million tweets over a 7.5 hour span. That's compared to 3.3 billion in 2014 over the course of 48 hours – clearly reaching way more people than pure user figures imply. That's a whole load of potential ad viewers that the advertising industry now knows just love entertainment shows.

"What's unique about it is that reach – what keeps Twitter relevant – is what people are coming into contact with it outside the platform," Stone adds. "That's also why Twitter has been making it a lot easier to explore that content – that's the interesting story."

Grow Your Twitter Account

Getting Noticed

Since there is a lot of activity happening on Twitter, the challenge is getting noticed and standing out. We showed you earlier how important it was to have a well crafted bio that sends the exact message you want to send. But having a nice looking bio and feed alone will not draw followers to you. You have to go out and get yourself noticed.

Here is a 5 step plan to getting noticed right away:

1. The first step is to know the type of followers you want to attract. The easy way to do this is to narrow down keywords that are related to the type of business you have.

2. From there, search those words using Twitter search. You can either search the top tweets or the latests tweets.

3. Scroll through and see the people who are talking about that term, and like every post that you find interesting. Then, search another term (with or without a hashtag) that interests you, and continue liking the tweets you like.

4. When you come across an account that you would like to follow, follow that account and comment on the tweet that you like.

5. As a test, attempt liking about 25-50 tweets and following 20-30 new accounts. Within a few hours, you should see some of the accounts returning the "like" that

you gave them. And you should also see that you've earned some new followers.

There are many reasons why doing this works. First, this works because when you like a tweet, you are getting the person who tweeted attention. The other reason why this is an effective strategy is because when you like a tweet, others who like the tweet after you see your profile.

You will also get the attention of the person who sent the tweet and their followers. The key is to get out and like every tweet that interests you. Do not be afraid to do this hundreds of times per day.

Twitter is a Conversation

Although Jack Dorsey has claimed in the past that Twitter is not a social media but instead is an media app, I would argue that not only is Twitter a social media platform, it is the only real social media platform out there. WIth all other platforms, the only way to connect with strangers that you have no relationship with is to comment or send them a direct message.

Of course, as we mentioned earlier, Twitter is the best news app on the planet. But the ability to follow anyone, and start a public or private conversation with anyone is special. What is even more special is the fact that anyone can listen in on those conversations. Even though Facebook and Instagram gives its users the ability to tag others in their posts, nobody carries on a conversation by posting on their post.

When you have a "connection and conversation" approach to Twitter, you begin to see its power.

Following and Following Back

Following a lot of users is another effective way to grow your following. Twitter has a daily cap on how many accounts you can follow per 24 hours. It has not been confirmed by Twitter. but it is believed that the cap is different for everyone. By most accounts, the maximum range is between 200-1,000 per day.

It is believed that accounts with higher following or a higher followers-to-following ratio also are able to follow more accounts. This means that if you are following 1,000 people but have 10,000 followers, you may be able to follow more accounts per day.

When using following as a strategy, be sure not to randomly follow all accounts or use auto-following robots. The reason you don't want to follow just anyone is because, again, your following count doesn't really matter if the people who are following you back are not really interested in what you have to say.

Instead, find someone who follows you and take a look at who they are following and who is following them. Visit those profiles that you are interested in and begin following those users. While you are checking out their profiles, a good way to engage is to like one of their tweets or retweet one of them. This should increase your follow back rate.

Just because you follow an account doesn't mean that you will get a follow back. A good followback percentage to shoot for is 30-40%. If you engage with each person you follow, you can increase your follow back percentage by 20-25%.

If your follow back percentage is consistently below 20%, it is time to stop and figure out why. Here are a few reasons why you may not be attracting the follow backs that you want. People think you're a robot

Twitter bots are a problem. These bots go out and follow accounts randomly or accounts that contain certain words or hashtags. You can often spot these bots because their feed, profile pictures, and bios are very unnatural. Without having a unique and personal touch to your account, some may see your account and lump you into the "bot" category.

Some Reasons Why They're Not Following You

No @conversations, no interactions

If your feed is a "broadcast-only feed," you are going to be seen as someone who talks but doesn't listen. Be sure that you are @mentioning and conversing with others. If you aren't replying to people who retweet you or @mention you, or you aren't starting conversations with interesting followers, you aren't maximizing on Twitter.

Too many retweets.

If your feed is all retweets and no original thoughts or conversation starters, you may lose some of your appeal. Retweeting is an important aspect of Twitter, but if you don't publish original thoughts and content, you lose some of your uniqueness.

Too self-serving/promotional

If you are only promoting your products and services, you may come off as too salesy. If you want people to follow you back, you've got to be a team player. This means not only linking to your own blog posts, products, and other things, but also sharing links that you find online or that your followers retweet.

Tweet Frequency

You need to tweet and tweet often. One thing you must remember about Twitter is that it is fast; very fast. Tweets move fast. The average life of a tweet is between 10 and 20 minutes. After that period of time, unless the tweet is retweeted or liked, most people will not see it unless they visit your feed.

Because of the speed of Twitter, in order to stay on the minds of the people who follow you, you must post more often than all other platforms. Only about 46% of Twitter users longin to the platform daily. This means on any given day, only about half of your followers are even going to login to Twitter.

What if you sent a tweet at 10 a.m. but every one of your followers decides to check their Twitter account at 6 p.m.?

Testing tweet frequency

So, I just spent the entire last section telling you why you should be tweeting more often. In this section, I'm going to show you why you shouldn't be going crazy and tweeting every minute of the day. Remember, you have to discover the ideal number of tweets for your audience and what is appropriate for the amount of followers you have.

As an account that has a large following, we are tweeting much more than most accounts. This is because we have a ton of content to share, and also because we want to reach as many people as possible. We have followers from all over the world, so we are tweeting at all hours of the day.

As a way to test our effectiveness, I decided that we should test to see what would happen if we tweeted less. After all, it always good to test your own assumptions and to not get comfortable with what has worked in the past. The idea was to tweet about 10% less than we previously had been.

The first thing we noticed was that traffic dropped. Which made sense; less tweet = less traffic. But after a while, the traffic seemed to return. Not all of it, but enough of it so that I didn't have to panic.

At the end of 28 days, I took a look at the stats and saw that there were a few key things that happened with our account. During the 28 day period, we sent out 1,071 tweets total, which was almost 11% less than our average. However, our total impressions increased by 4.5% to a total of 997,000 impressions.

Also, the amount of "@Startupmindset" mentions increased as well by 4.6%. That means that more people were sharing our content on Twitter with our handle. That might have been due to retweets.

It is worth noting that some of those mentions could have been from visitors coming to our site from other sources and then sharing the content on Twitter on their own using our social share toolbar. When that happens, @Startupmindset is included in the tweet. Either way, it was a good thing for us.

We did, however, notice a few metrics that declined during the 28 day period. An important one was profile visits. We saw a nearly 19% decline in visitors to our profile. This means that there were fewer people viewing our profile and feed. We also saw a decrease in new followers in this particular period of time.

Account home

StartUp Mindset @StartUpMindset

28 day summary with change over previous period

Tweets	Tweet impressions	Profile visits	Mentions
1,071 ↓11.4%	997K ↑4.5%	5,202 ↓18.6%	274 ↑4.6%

So what should you do with information? Even though there are several other tests that we would run, this little bit of information was helpful. With this information, we understood when we should tweet often and when we should scale it back.

It seems that when we want engagement and want our posts to be seen by more people, we should decrease the amount of tweets we are sending per day. Tweeting 10% less increased our engagement, which helps future tweets be seen by the people who engaged with us.

But, when we want to spike our following to increase and want our profile to receive more visits, we should be tweeting more.

You should be testing your tweeting frequency often. Algorithms change, as well as the behaviors of your followers and your potential followers. Continue to test the amount of tweets as well as when you tweet them.

Final Thoughts

Not every business should seek a massive following. However, if you want to build any type of personal brand, not having a Twitter presence may be a mistake. It is easier to deliver thoughts to the masses via Twitter than any other platform. Learn to converse on the platform, and watch your influence grow.

CHAPTER 7
CONNECT ON LINKEDIN

"If what you are doing doesn't add value, they won't listen to you."

-*Marcus Sheridan*

LinkedIn is the foremost community of professionals in the world. As a tool for recruiting, it's unparalleled but it also serves a greater function. A robust presence on LinkedIn with meaningful content creation and engagement with other businesses can help your business to connect with like-minded professionals, potential mentors, and to identify sales leads.

Whether you are a recent graduate, have spent a few years in an industry, or are closer to retirement than not, having a solid LinkedIn page is a great way to connect with your peers and to grow your social presence. LinkedIn takes elements from traditional social media networks, <u>such as the newsfeed</u>, connection requests based on mutual acceptances, and a customizable profile, and imbues them with a strong networking platform and job posting board.

Users have the ability to create and act as the administrator of their own small business's page, or to create their own profile as an individual. Individual profiles work hand in hand with company profiles, as the two can interact with each other, and direct traffic back to the other through links and branded content.

Managing an individual page

As users connect with other users, their network grows and offers new opportunities to engage and market. Savvy LinkedIn members are wise about who they connect with. LinkedIn encourages users to connect virtually with colleagues, acquaintances, and business contacts rather than with strangers, which helps to facilitate the networking aspect of the platform.

On your own individual page, it's wise to link your education and experience back to the universities and corporations that you reference. These linkages add credibility to your page and act as a sort of internal SEO that boosts your profile when other users search for that organization.

An individual LinkedIn profile acts as a virtual resume, business card, and elevator pitch for yourself all in one. Adding a recent headshot, updating the profile when you receive a promotion or switch to a new position, and connecting with new contacts are all great ways to keep your profile looking its best and serving its ultimate networking function.

Using a company page

Small businesses and startups can also benefit from hosting their own company page. Here, you can post content about your business, post jobs and search for candidates, and grow a follower base that can be targeted as sales prospects.

Your company page will likely be built with similar content that you use on your website. Adding a photo of your company's logo and a cover image will bring your page to life. LinkedIn states that companies that use their logo as their page photo drive six times more traffic. Using social media badges, you can link your LinkedIn to your website and vice versa, helping to drive traffic to both.

Content Marketing is Key
Content is ultimately what will build up your LinkedIn following to your company's page. Your

content should be written for your target audience, not for the LinkedIn community at large. If you are a data visualization firm, post content on that subject rather than on some topic that is currently trending. Daily content is ideal, but posting once a week is a good benchmark.

Your content should be engaging, appeal to your target customers, and inform your readers about both the issue at hand and position you as a trustworthy thought leader and subject matter expert. If you have great content that you want to boost, you can pay to sponsor your content and extend its reach to new viewers, much like sponsored posts on other social media sites.

<u>Optimize the headlines</u> and keywords of your posts, and link them back to your other sites. <u>Driving earned media</u> through your own channels is a highly effective marketing technique and can drive your customers to your ecommerce platforms, if relevant to your business.

As with other social media platforms, you will want to spend time each week engaging with your followers, monitoring interactions, and making yourself available to answer any customer questions and concerns. You have the ability to track and monitor engagement with your page through LinkedIn analytics. Set goals for your page, just as you would with any of your other digital marketing channels, and assess your progress periodically.

Your company page adds credibility and trust to your brand. Millions of LinkedIn users engage with companies and brands every day, and you miss out on these engagements and potential sales opportunities by failing to update your page and posting content.

LinkedIn is also a great recruiting tool. The majority of LinkedIn's user base are white collar, skilled workers and tend to skew towards higher socioeconomic statuses and education attainment levels. Niche industries and mega corporations alike post jobs on LinkedIn's job board and attract interest from a varied base of applicants.

LinkedIn is a great way to stay connected to your professional contacts, to grow your base of sales leads and targets, and to establish you and your brand as thought leaders in your category. Keep in mind that LinkedIn is a professional site, and that what you post has the potential to reach more than 500 million users around the world.

The networking opportunities are endless with a site like LinkedIn, but be thoughtful and err on the side of professionalism when it comes to accepting invitations to connect and sending out your own invitations, particularly if you are not acquaintances with the individual. Keeping your profiles up to date with important news and engaging content is the best way to attract followers and grow your network.

CHAPTER 8

BEATING NEWSFEED ALGORITHMS

"I get 100% open rate', said no one ever."
-*Mari Smith*

Newsfeed algorithms are a friend and enemy to us who would like to use social media to generate more leads and produce a larger circle of influence. The algorithms help identify the individuals who may benefit most from what we have to offer. However, they limit how many of those individuals actually see what we present.

It can be frustrating to see that something you've spent a lot of time and energy producing, doesn't even reach 10% of the people who could be interested in seeing your work. However, algorithm changes are a part of our lives now so the best we can do is to understand them and learn how to use them to our advantage.

In this chapter, we won't get technical about how to beat newsfeed algorithms. Instead, one of our writers, Sadia, has some things she'd like to share on the topic of newsfeed algorithms and some tips on how you can increase your visibility.

The rest of this chapter was written by Sadia as she tells her story of dealing with the many changes of newsfeed algorithms and what you can do to beat them.

Beating Newsfeed algorithms

While out to dinner last night, I noticed that my friends had developed a "Snapchat tendency." I watched patiently as each one painstakingly chronicled our outing by posting a snap as we entered the dumpling joint, ordered, waited, and then ate the said dumplings!

Trying to stick to my New Year's resolution (thou shall not judge others unjustly – or something like that), I decided not to admonish my friends and instead came away from the night with a new-found appreciation for Snapchat. True to its original premise, "snaps" are instantaneously broadcast to one's subscribers/ followers/friends (?) without any hassle of ranking algorithms (that other sites have started using).

After coming to an agonizing conclusion last year that my life wasn't cool enough to be broadcasted 24/7, I had decided to refrain from Snapchat, and instead focus my energies on sustaining at least three social media accounts: Facebook, Instagram, and Twitter.

I didn't want to overwhelm myself with yet another social media account as well. But lately, my chosen three platforms' convoluted newsfeed/timeline setup has started to irk me.

There are all sets of rules for increasing engagement and viewership of one's posts on these sites, with each platform suggesting a different set of them. **Yikes!** I was starting to think that maybe it was time for me to give up on social media altogether when I remembered my other New Year's resolution: "thou shall not give up easily – or something like that." **I decided to take a stand, and crack down on those ranking algorithms before quitting on social media.** This is what I came up with.

Algorithmic Ranking

Most social media sites today use a combination of algorithms to "rank" stories in users' newsfeeds through a set of criteria. They have abandoned the chronological dissemination of information in favor of this method, arguing that the new formulas afford its users a more personalized experience. These "artificially placed" posts occupy the first dozen slots on our homepages.

As a result, us users are fed the most-relevant information that is guaranteed to get a reaction out of us: a like, a comment, or a share. Our reactions to posts are known as "<u>post engagements</u>," and it is estimated that 10% of original posters' posts are seen, while post engagements come from a mere 2% of the post's viewers.

It doesn't feed into social media sites' interests if you, as the user, don't react to things or don't engage with posts. **When you do nothing, then you are not contributing any information about yourself to the site.** It serves the site's interests to keep us coming back to the site every day and contributing large chunks of information to them. From these large data sets, the sites can then ascertain our likes, dislikes, and interests, and eventually what sort of marketing material would appeal to us.

Thus, all roads lead to ad revenues. Remember, **"if it's free then you are the product being sold."** Facebook has built its business by being a necessity in our daily lives. The site takes up 50 minutes (up from 40 minutes last year) of our day every day (on average), and the company generates some $1 billion in revenues. Surely, they're doing something right! Not only do they want you going back every day, but they also want to make sure that you spend more and more time there each day as well. Simply put, more time every day equals more money. **Hence, the diabolical game of newsfeed ranking was born.**

Other sites such as Twitter and Instagram are also known to artificially re-arrange our newsfeeds as well. Owned by Facebook, Instagram has truly blossomed into the new darling of <u>online marketing</u>, but unfortunately Twitter does not share the same fortune. Twitter users are spending less than one minute on average on the site every day, thus its ranking algorithms aren't doing much for them.

How to Beat the Rankings and Build Organic Reach

My main gripe with newsfeed ranking is that it does not always get my posts to the relevant audience, nor does it give them the right reach. Yes, I understand that AI and machine-learning is not perfect and that over time it will improve, but that won't stop me from complaining!

This brings to question, "so how do these sites 'rank' our newsfeeds anyway, and how do we bring those AI bots in our favor?"

The end goal is to make ourselves more visible to the relevant audience, and to do so, you need to know what are the ranking criteria of social media sites.

Quality of Content

I have a niggling disdain for those who prefer binging on buffets to eating at specialty restaurants. I have always held a firm belief in "quality over quantity," and it seems that social media sites do too.

The likes of Facebook and Twitter are known to penalize you if you post regularly or "spam" users' feeds. They will rank major posts – such as a wedding picture or an engagement announcement – higher in the ranking table because it is a "major life event," i.e., if it is "quality content." Quality content can also mean the "most popular post" of your many posts (if you post frequently) – this is the post with the highest engagement.

Friends and families' posts are always shown higher in the newsfeed than "Liked" pages/business' posts on both Facebook and Instagram. This is because 1) we tend to prefer viewing and reacting to friends and families' posts over business' ones, and 2) because business pages post much too frequently.

Facebook and Instagram don't want to bombard us with business' minute-by-minute posts, thus "Liked" pages undergo the highest amount of scrutiny in their ranking calculations.

Sadly, Twitter does not always have that ability, because users are known to subscribe to news outlets on Twitter more than friends and families' Twitter profiles. This could be another reason why Twitter lags in revenue generation.

Relationship/History with User/Viewer

On Facebook, you are likely to feature higher on another user's homepage based on your relationship with him or her. You will firstly outweigh "Liked" pages by being on someone's friend list, but because users nowadays have 600+ friends on average, you will secondly have to compete with those 600-other people. What comes into factor then is whether (or not) you regularly interact with the potential post-viewer on the site.

If you are a "passive friend" on the post viewer's friend list, then you will not rank highly on their newsfeeds. If you do however interact heavily with him/her via messaging and other post engagements, then you can climb the ranks on their newsfeed and vice versa. "Passive friends" posts do feature highly on newsfeeds if it is a "quality content" post or a "major event" post.

Meanwhile, Twitter and Instagram both struggle to ascertain "real accounts" to "business accounts," and it is unclear if they rank friends and families' posts higher on their newsfeeds than businesses' posts. Instead, Twitter and Instagram employs the "viral rule" meaning that posts with more engagement showcase higher on newsfeeds than posts with little or no engagement

Posting Frequency and Time of Posting

Social media guru, Neil Patel, says that one of the keys to building a followership on social media is finding the right balance of post frequency (this hearkens back to the quantity over quality rule). He also argues that there happens to be an exact science for the number of times you should post in every platform, while making sure to post only when most of your potential post-viewers are online.

It is universally accepted that three tweets per day bring in more post-engagement than any fewer tweets. It is also somehow believed that two posts per day on Facebook is the golden rule for high post-engagement, but that is only applicable if you already have a large audience. The optimal number of Facebook posts is up for debate, as gurus suggest employing a trial-and-error method to crack the code.

Meanwhile, it is generally frowned upon when Instagram users post many back-to-back pictures on the portal, thus it is suggested that spacing out the posts over the span of some hours is always a good practice. One post per day is good enough for Instagram in general.

The "life-cycle" of a story or post is longer for Facebook at 90 minutes, whereas on Twitter, it is 24 minutes. What this means is that tweets posted within the last 24 minutes are high on the ranking cue and post-24 minutes, their position on the ranking table declines. Facebook meanwhile holds posts with more levity for a longer period than Twitter. This metric perfectly sums up why Twitter requires more posts than Facebook and Instagram combined.

In Conclusion

That's it for my rant on the social media sites' sinister newsfeed/timeline ranking tendencies, and how we can vigilantly fight for our space on the Internet. Good luck navigating them!

CHAPTER 9

SELLING THROUGH STORYTELLING

"Sometimes reality is too complex. Stories give it form."

-*Jean Luc Godard*

With a following of almost 2 million people across Instagram, Facebook, Twitter, and Snapchat, Cynthia Johnson knows a lot about influencing, branding, and the art of storytelling. Cynthia is a business advisor, author, and CEO and Co-Founder of Bell + Ivy, a digital marketing and personal branding agency in Santa Monica, CA.

She is also on the Forbes Agency Council, a member of the Young Entrepreneurs Council and has written for and been interviewed on topics such as entrepreneurship, brand management and digital marketing in publications such as Forbes, Huffington Post, Inc., and Chicago Planner Magazine.

I had the pleasure of interviewing Cynthia for an article we entitled Expert Storytelling, Brand Advancement, and Influencing Millions: Our Interview with Cynthia Johnson (https://startupmindset.com/expert-storytelling-brand-advancement-and-influencing-millions-our-interview-with-cynthia-johnson/). In the interview, Cynthia shared the unique skill of successful storytelling and how the ability to tell your story is the key to gaining influence.

I asked Cynthia what advice she would give to entrepreneurs who are running a startup that is in the survival stage of the business cycle and would like to advance to the success stage. Part of her answer was to tell your story in a way that is easy to understand. **"Explain your company to a three-year-old and keep doing that in various ways until that 3-year old understands what you are talking about"**.

She went on to talk about what it really means to be influential on social media and how she approached the idea of gaining influence. "Growing your influence is about listening to people and deliverable something of value", she says. **"You have to create a place where people can learn something, communicate, and feel like there is something to gain by paying attention to you.** The truth is that everyone has influence – the more people you influence- the greater the responsibility and the more you have to work".

To Cynthia and many others who use social media to drive their businesses, influence is all about the story you tell and keep telling. The reason why many long-time entrepreneurs who have offline businesses struggle to increase sales using social media is not because of the medium, it is because they haven't learned how to tell their story the right way, to the right people.

Who are you and why should I buy from you?

As a small business or startup looking to sell on social media, the method of doing so often gets muddy. Many entrepreneurs often look at larger and more established companies and try to duplicate what is working for those companies. That may be effective in some ways, but on social media, doing what the big guys do is not always the best option.

Larger companies have the been around for a while have the benefit of branding, distribution, and massive marketing dollars behind them. When it comes to selling their products and services on social media, larger companies tap into the resources that are already at their disposal. As a startup or small business, you have to use what you do have in order to compete.

Lucky for you, when selling on social media, it is not only about what is for sale, it is about who is selling it. The one buying habit that has been created by social media is the habit of investigating the seller. If you were to walk into a Wal-Mart or target to buy paper towels, it is unlikely that you would stop and Google the story of how Wal-Mart got started or even the maker of the paper towels. Most likely you are going to look at the price, quality, and brands available before you purchase.

When purchasing from retail stores like Wal-Mart, Target, and even Amazon, most consumers are more concerned with the product, what it does, and is it the right price. On social media, the perfect product could be presented to a qualified buyer but that buyer may not buy if they are unfamiliar with the seller.

The mistake most entrepreneurs make when trying to drive sales on social media is that the focus too much on what they are selling. The present the benefits and the solutions their product or services will solve. This is a great sales tactic in many scenarios, but on social media, it is not as effective as selling your story first.

In an upcoming interview on StartUp Mindset, we will be featuring Dr. Brynn Windgard. Dr. Brynn Winegard is an award-winning professor, speaker, and expert. She performs keynote speeches on how leaders can "build a better business brain". During one of her keynotes, she explains why trying to sell using facts, data, and information is not effective.

She explains that most decisions that are made by the human brain are subconscious decisions. The actual percentage is not known for every human but it is safe to say 90-95% of the brain is operating on a subconscious level. When selling, it is best to try to speak to the subconscious minds of your potential clients, not their conscious minds.

Like we mentioned earlier in this book, social media platforms were designed with social interaction in mind. Most people to go to Twitter, Facebook, or Instagram to purchase something. They go to connect to that desire their subconscious is looking to fulfill. They are going there in order to connect.

Your goal is to give them someone to connect with. You want to sell to them you must connect with them with your ability to tell meaningful stories. You must be able to tell them who you are in a way that is captivating, unique, and relevant to them and also connects them with your business.

The Art of Storytelling

An idea doesn't sell itself. Your product can have all the qualities that make it better than others, it can be innovative, and different, but if you don't know how to communicate a vision properly, whether it is to customers or a potential investor, it won't be enough.

For people, experiences matter. Due to the advent of technology and the massive rise over the last decade and a half of social media, the focus in advertising and marketing a product has shifted away from facts in order to encompass an entire universe of human experiences. How you bridge the gap between your product and these experiences is imperative.

So why does a good story sell and how do you make sure you are using the proper tools to communicate with your audience?

So why does a good story sell and how do you make sure you are using the proper tools to communicate with your audience?

Storytelling is an inherent part of human nature

From the dawn of time, people have developed different methods of telling stories in order to communicate, create, and more specifically compel others to act. No matter what the underlying goal of your startup is, there are aspects of the human condition that you must consider when building your message.

This rhetoric is present in many of the ad campaigns you see on a daily basis walking down the street or zapping through Youtube videos. This is because digging into the most important parts of the human psyche by asking the right questions about the audience you want to reach is how you can understand what people truly want.

The reality is most of the things we buy and use nowadays are beyond the realm of what we would call "basic necessities". Let's take the smartphone craze as an example. You don't need a smartphone with fifty-thousand applications so why do you still want it? What has made it evolve from a luxury to a necessity?

Well, it's as simple as the story that is written with invisible ink on the fabric of the product. It is about connecting to emotions, finding out what makes all human beings tick and turn their heads; it goes far beyond the necessity of a product based solely on its qualities but rather into the need to identify with something bigger than ourselves. To find authentic meaning in the products we buy.

How, where, and when you tell your story is important. There are many factors to consider when selling your story, factors that make it a full-bodied experience. Thanks to social media platforms and a massively developed online community it has become much more feasible to get your message across in a low-cost, multi-mediated way.

Still, knowing what you want to convey (vision) and who you want to convey it to (target audience) is the first step to creating that message.

Be creative when drafting a story, but don't drift too far away from home

What do I mean by this? Think of the feelings and experiences we all share, those that are linked to emotion; the taste of a home-cooked meal, getting to see a friend who is far away, the sound of laughter coming from a child and the distinct smell of the person you love. The stories that linger are those which are conveyed by calling on the senses.

Of course, one thing entrepreneurs must always remember is to make sure all aspects of their story are in sync: whatever social media platforms they choose to use, the talking points that move their message forward in front of an audience, even the basic aspects of images and videos, have to be coherently produced. Framing the who, what, and how of your vision within a "story bubble" of this sort will give your message credibility and substance.

Involving people in the stories is also important. Letting them share, **making them feel as though they are part of this bigger picture** you are trying to create can be easily done through social media. After all, this is what the online community is all about, sharing experiences; we all want to be part of the bigger picture.

Think of hashtags, likes, shares, images contests, influencers, and all the little nuances of social media as your own virtual messenger pigeons. They will carry your story across platforms. It is important that your vision is whole, so that when it is carried around it can be easily recognized.

Lastly, consider the WHEN as your biggest ally
Timing comes in two forms: knowing when to publish a message, and being aware of what is going on around you when you do. For the first, think technically, it's all about knowing your audience; for example, when are they most likely to see your message on any given social media platform?

In terms of the second "type" of timing, being aware means not losing any opportunity to tie current events to your story, but also being conscious of the temporal context in which you plan to place your message. Don't forget that you are still promoting your idea. Your ultimate goal is to not lose your message while aiding it with things that are seemingly relevant in today's world. Storytelling is an undying art that can be and should be, applied to any vision.

Entrepreneurs should remember that what matters the most is the authenticity of the story. To put it briefly, first you have to sell the experience, then you can sell the product. It's all about inspiring different audiences through stories that move them and that they can connect with.

CHAPTER 10

SELLING USING CONTENT

"You can buy attention (advertising). You can beg for attention from the media (PR). You can bug people one at a time to get attention (sales). Or you can earn attention by creating something interesting and valuable and then publishing it online for free."

-David Meerman Scott

In 1995, Bill Gates said that, "Content is King." That was over 20+ years ago (my heart be still), but Mr. Gates was spot on. As the Internet evolved and influenced an entire generation, content marketing evolved in a way that many businesses never saw coming. The term, "social media," is now everyday jargon, and businesses who do not invest it can find themselves in more trouble than they realize.

At one time, Facebook (or FaceSpace as my grandma says) and Twitter were just social platforms for people to connect with friends. They have now become crucial hubs for potential customers and clients alike. To ignore that could be the beginning of the end in a way you never saw coming.

As a Millennial, I am going to share **five of the most important reasons why businesses fail when not utilizing content marketing in this present day**.

1. People look to the Internet for a company's information (goodbye phonebook)

I know that when I need to look up a phone number for a business, I immediately pull out my phone to find their information on Google. I can't even remember the last time that I pulled out a phone book (do I still get them?) to lookup someone's number. Having a website in the Internet world to place your company's information is critical for many people.

I always look up a website's "About us" and "services" pages before I do business with them. When businesses choose to not have a website on who they are and what they offer, then their relevance drops for me. In a way, if you don't exist online, then you simply don't exist at all.

2. We are a visual society – the fewer words, the better

According to website, t-sciences.com, "The human brain processes images 60,000 times faster than text, and 90% of information transmitted to the brain is visual." As the saying goes, a picture is worth a thousand words. Your content doesn't have to be endless word vomit, but a simple picture that says something in a way that thousands of words simply couldn't.

Social media platforms such as Instagram, Pinterest, and Facebook offer ways to share photos and videos in ways you never could before. Content doesn't just encompass words anymore. In limiting yourself to just that avenue, you are missing a vast audience of young consumers who could easily grow your business.

3. Social media reaches people you wouldn't normally reach

I cannot tell you how many times I have seen people ask for recommendations online when it comes to certain skills or trades. Many people respond with their preferences and tag the company's online profile for easy access. This is great for Millennials, and other online consumers, who want easy and simple when it comes to reaching a business.

Social media platforms also reach people who you couldn't have 20 years ago. Shopping based websites, such as Etsy, have helped elevate businesses from a local level, to national and international retailers. As a business owner, recognizing that there is more out there than just your local community could be essential to your success. In contrast, being scared to go out of your comfort zone could be more detrimental to your business than you realize.

4. Competition is out there – keep your content fresh and updated

While it would be nice to think that you are the only one in your field, it is probably not the case for most businesses. To utilize defunct, or practically extinct ways of content marketing, <u>could give your competition a lead in obtaining potential customers</u>. Make sure you are up-to-date on the popular social media platforms that best suit your kind of business endeavor.

If you are not sure which ones would work best for your company's needs, just do some research or check out a competitor's online profiles. From there, you can figure out which route you want to take when updating your content.

If you are leery of social media, or don't know where to start, hire someone who can help with this business realm. Many Millennials, myself included, would love a chance to help someone with their social media accounts. You can also offer internships for local college kids who want experience in this type of field. This is not only good for them, but also for your company in getting your content marketing updated to the 21st century.

5. If you don't control the image of your company, others will

People will talk. You can't control that. However, you can control the response and image of your company by being in the forefront of gossip and other talk. Having a Facebook page, a website "contact us" page, or other social media pages can give your audience an easy route to reach you. When you ignore these mediums, people will go to other online avenues to vent their frustrations or share positive experiences.

Interaction is also key with your audience. Regardless of whether you get <u>good or bad reviews</u>, you should be the one in control of your businesses' image and reputation. People like to be heard and feel like they matter to a company. If they invest in you, you should also invest and care about them. That is why you must be on top of your company's reputation, both online and in person. Businesses that fail to recognize that will soon realize the errors of their ways, but it may already be too late.

Hopefully, this helps shed light on important ways to manage your content outside of the "old school" ways. Be open, adaptable, and remember that content is king, both online and in person. Understanding what content to present to audience can be what makes or breaks your business. Do not be afraid of the digital world, because it's not nearly as scary as a "Going out of Business" sign.

What you may be doing wrong

Every marketing expert, guru, and website has repeatedly told you that content marketing is one of the best ways to give your business exposure online. So, you build a blog, share information on social media, and even begin creating videos in order to put yourself and your business out there to the world.

But content marketing can be tricky especially to a newcomer. Since the internet is just one big piece of content, standing out in a sea of information is tough. There are a ton of mistakes you can make when executing a content marketing plan. Those mistakes waste valuable time, energy, money, and other resources.

To make sure you are you are getting the most out of your content marketing, here are 5 of the most common mistakes to avoid making when you launch a content marketing campaign.

Mistakes you're making with your content marketing

Your content isn't good enough

Yes, it's true that we entrepreneurs have a problem with perfectionism. But some entrepreneurs go in the exact opposite direction and don't take the time to create content that is above average. If you don't produce content that is valuable enough to grab people's attention you're never going to get the exposure you need.

Content is a commodity online. In order to stand out from the crowd, you must take the time and energy to create videos, articles, and images that are unique and encourages your consumers to engage. Great content also helps your [business website rank higher](#) with the search engines like Yahoo and Google. The higher you rank, the more people will find you.

If you are producing a video, make sure that it doesn't look like everything else that is on Youtube and Facebook.

If Twitter is your primary marketing platform, be sure that you are sharing your best work and are not just delivering generic tweets to your followers. Even your Instagram account should be unique and dynamic enough in order to differentiate yourself from the herd. Make sure that your content is unique, helpful, and keeps the consumer in mind.

Your blog posting isn't consistent

A sure fire way to reach any goal is to be consistent in your actions. Whether it's weight loss or your marketing strategy, effective and consistent actions will yield results. The problem is that most entrepreneurs are not consistent with their marketing activities.

According to Curata, <u>70% of marketers lack consistency</u> in their content marketing. That's a huge number! No matter how good your marketing plan is, it will fail if it is not well executed. If you are running a blog, having a posting schedule is the key to ensuring that your readers have reasons to keep coming back to your blog.

Your social media profiles should be updated frequently in order for your followers to remember you. The lifespan of the average tweet is 20 minutes. That means you should be tweeting at least once a day in order to be in the forefront of your reader's minds. Whether it is blogging, email marketing, or social media posting, be sure to be consistent in all of your actions.

Your content lacks variety

Video is becoming the hot format when it comes to content marketing. However, it is too early to know if the trend towards video will eclipse text and image marketing. Even though <u>85% of Youtube and Facebook</u> users watch an hour of video per week, many people still prefer to consume content via the written word or through infographics.

The key is to give people a variety of options. Mixing video, text, and images will ensure that your audience gets to choose how they consume the content you deliver. Keep in mind that you must still keep the level of quality consistent no matter what type of content you are sharing.

You're not repurposing your content

One of the obstacles that most content producers face is the question of what they should post. It can get exhausting trying to produce new content for your followers daily. That is why it is a good idea to repurpose your content periodically in order to save yourself some time and effort.

The article you produce for your business blog can also be shared on Linkedin and a blogging platform like Medium since those platforms respond well to text articles. You can also create a video of yourself discussing the topic and post it on Facebook and Youtube. You do not need to write new content, you just need to offer a video version of the article you've already written.

You may also want to share old content with your new followers. Twitter is a great platform to do this on. Like I mentioned before, tweets have a short lifespan if they do not go viral. Because of this, you may be able to share the same blog post, video, or message several times per week especially if you have a growing audience.

Your headlines need work

You may have awesome content, a mix of video and text, and even a consistent posting schedule, but if you do not have compelling headlines, no one will care. Having a <u>dynamic headline</u> is the key to clickthroughs and engagement.

Think about all of the times you clicked on an article because of the headline or opened an email because of the subject line. If you need help coming up with a headline, using tools such as <u>The Impact Blog Title Generator</u> from BlogAbout or <u>The Blog Title Generator</u> are a good place to start.

It is, however, very important that you don't produce clickbait headlines. Be very careful not to mislead or consumers into clicking a piece of content and not meeting their expectation. This will not only cause them to immediately click the back button, but it will tarnish your credibility for future posts.

In the next chapter, we'll show you how to write attention getting headlines that will stand out.

CHAPTER 11

WRITING ATTENTION GETTING HEADLINES

"When you can do the common things of life in an uncommon way, you will command the attention of the world."

-*George Washington Carver*

If you've created a high-quality article, video or images that took hours of your time, you really hope that it will engage your readers. Here's the scenario. You excitedly click "post" and incessantly check to see how many likes and shares you receive. The usual fans click 'like' right away which you appreciate, of course.

The thing is you're looking for more engagement. You want shares and hundreds of likes for your hard work. When that doesn't happen, you may feel like it was for nothing. Something you may not realize is your titles may be falling short which is the most important part of your whole post.

With so much information online, readers are usually browsing headlines. If something hits them, something that may have kept them awake at night, they will click and read. While you may feel skeptical about the power of headlines, it's been backed by science. Based on statistics, your headline is the largest influence on how much traffic you'll receive. It's more important than the post itself. If you create captivating headlines, you stand to increase your rankings immediately. You will be able to grab the attention of your readers even through all the other posts out there.

Consider Who You Want to Attract

While it's a nice thought to create a headline that will attract everyone, it's more important to have a relevant reader. It's better known as your target audience. An audience that will become engaged with your post.

They may become a customer or client of yours because what you have is what they want. This is an important foundation to creating posts and headlines effectively. Hopefully, you know who your target audience is. If you know who they are, consider what their obsessions are.

What do Your Readers Want?

If you can figure out what your readers really want, you'll have plenty of <u>brilliant ideas</u> for headlines as well as content. Your readers want something tangible from you. Think about a friend who has exciting news about their life. What is it that makes their day? What makes your day? Some general things that excite people are;

- A promotion

- Making a sale on their first product or service

- Getting into a relationship

- Gaining a new client

- Losing weight

With these examples in mind, you could create headlines that promise to help them get these desires. The headline is the promise while the content, video or images fulfill that promise.

- 7 Secrets to Getting a Promotion

- How to Sell Your First Product Easily

- 9 Ways to Attract Your Soulmate

- How to Show a Potential Client that You're the Right Fit

- Lose 10 Pounds in 20 Days While Still Enjoying Donuts

The How-to Headline

Can't you just see it now? Your post retweeted thousands of times and shared all over Facebook? The power of how-to articles has been monitored on the blogosphere. Results showed that these types of articles were the most prominent in the shared and liked department. This is because you're delivering a promise with this style of headline.

Another bonus of a how-to headline is it's a great guideline to deliver the information you've promised in the headline. Keep this in mind, people don't want to learn how to do more. What they want is to seek out tips and tricks they can use to make life easier and for them to feel happier about themselves. There are a wide variety of how-to headline formulas out there.

Here are some great samples;
- How to Increase Sales and Get Rich (this is a double how to with similar promises, one leading

to the next)

- How I Made a Fortune While Eating Potato Chips

- How One Simple Thought Can Change the Success of Your Business

Listicle Headline Formats

So with your target market in mind, consider what do your readers have to know in order to improve their lives? A headline that lists various reasons, secrets or styles so people can obtain their desires is golden.

They just want to experience concrete information on self improvement in the simplest way possible.
For example, if you're offering a course on how to make money online, effective headlines can include;

- How to Make Money Online (Even if You've Never Clicked a Mouse)

- 7 Secrets that Will Allow You to Quit Your Job this Year

- How to Quit Your Job and Make the Same Amount of Money

Who Else Wants?

This style of headline is an excellent strategy specifically for social media platforms. You are already implying that you know how to achieve a desire that many of your readers are also seeking. It has been used a lot with internet marketing but not so much with other industries.
Here are some examples;

- Who Else Wants Great Hair with Little Hassle?

- Who Else Wants a Free Holiday to a Warm Place this Winter?

- Who Else Wants Pet Food that Makes their Dog Healthier?

Using Power Words

Another important aspect to creating a headline that will be noticed on social media is to evoke emotion. One of the best ways to achieve that takes just one power word. They can make all the difference on whether you gain attention to your post.
Here are some examples which are divided into

Fears; agony, danger, toxic and victim

Make us feel alive; amazing, conquer, magic and stunning

Anger; abuse, lies, punish and ruthless

Greed; free, frenzy, profit and rich

Safe feeling words; guaranteed, no risk, research and tested and proven

Here's a real statistic that should motivate you into curating awesome headlines. On average, 8 out of 10 people will read your headline while just 2 out of 10 will read what follows. People have so much information thrown at them daily that they have developed filters.

Spelling out the specific benefits they will get by reading more is where your power lies. Engaging readers to respond to your posts will make them feel emotional about it. This is why they'll pass it onto others. The headline is the first step to getting noticed and when you create it, make sure you deliver the promises in the body of the post.

CHAPTER 12

USING INFLUENCERS TO SPIKE YOUR BRAND

"Sometimes, if you want to change a man's mind, you have to change the mind of the man next to him first."
— *Megan Whalen Turner,*
from the book The King of Attolia

Most startups won't be able to afford traditional celebrity endorsements of their products, but the widespread use of social media has allowed new classes of influencers, including micro-influencers, to gain marketing power.

Social media influencers feature your products or brand in their posts and help you reach larger audiences. Social media influencers often have well-defined niches and specialties to help your brand get recognized by the very people who would be most interested in it.

What You Need to Know about Influencer Marketing

Influencer marketing combines word-of-mouth endorsement with trusted referrals and reviews to help brands gain exposure in the crowded world of social media. Influencer marketing includes social media influencers, bloggers, brand ambassadors or advocates, niche promoters, and YouTube stars who create content to develop awareness and facilitate sales. Influencers are frequently active on a few social media platforms or have a much-followed blog.

Finding the correct influencers for your brand could mean big Return on Investment (ROI) and powerful branding partnerships.

Why Influencers?

Among the influencers' greatest attributes is a wide network. But an influencer's reach is not only measured by their followers. If an influencer has done a good job of <u>engaging followers</u> and fellows, then there's a good chance that they will also be able to communicate with their followers' networks, meaning an even wider audience for your products and services.

Customers are more likely to trust recommendations from a third party than from the brand itself. Influencers can make a brand seem more personal by integrating your brand into their lifestyle and blogging routines. Rather than relying on a few high budget ads that they disseminate to many outlets, influencers grow their audience's trust through consistent, quality posting.

Influencer marketing isn't necessarily flying under the radar, as far as marketing goes. Customers know about influencers, and the FTC has been cracking down on paid influencer posts that go unmarked. Nonetheless, most customers are more likely to trust influencer posts than ads and posts that are marked as sponsored content. Furthermore, customers elect to follow influencers, read their posts, and watch their videos, making it their choice to see these particular advertisements.

Influencer Market Goals
Like any other marketing strategy, your influencer marketing needs a story and an aim. Ask yourself why you need your influencer. Are you intending to drive sales? Or simply looking to accumulate followers and <u>brand awareness</u>?

You should then define what kind of reach your ideal influencer would have. Are they a blogger? Instagram user? Pinterest? Twitter? Or are you intending to generate content across multiple platforms? YouTube is a great way to reach the teenage audience, while Facebook has more appeal for professional-aged to older generations.

Successful influencers can drive traffic to your website, grow your brand's social media profile, develop branded hashtags for you, and in some cases, they will flat out sell your products.

Your ideal influencer will push past brand awareness by giving their audience a call to action about your product. More than just visiting a location or using a product, the influencer will make their audiences want to visit that location or use that product. They can help you orchestrate sales and promotions, giveaways, and demonstrate ways of making your products and services applicable to their audience.

Your Ideal Influencer
To find the best influencer for your brand, think about the type of accounts and personalities that your audience would follow. You can start by searching the hashtags that these accounts would generally use.

Niche is everything. Influencers in your niche will already be generating content that is similar to your brand. They might also be taking part in conversations about you and your competitors. Engaging influencers and <u>creating brand loyalty</u> among them is a good way of steering niche-based conversation favorably in your direction.

Influencers have their own form of branding, so not every influencer will work for your brand. The reach of their audience is not enough to sell your products. Their audience must also connect with the products or services that the influencer is featuring.

Middle-range influencers, or micro-influencers, are people who average between 10k and 100k followers. These will be your best bet for most brands, because they have a wide reach while still being small enough to engage with their followers and cultivate loyalty on a personal level.

What are the Risks?

Any influencer that you hire will most likely post about other things than your brand. This is risky, because these other things your influencer posts could positively or negatively reflect on your brand. Some influencers, especially those trying to expand their reach, will do a lot just to get clicks, likes, and attention. Influencer marketing forms a partnership between brands in some cases, and the influencer's exposure will feed on your brand. If your influencer posts something that is distasteful, it could implicate your brand and cause you a headache while you explain your way out of working with that influencer.

You might also lose some control over how your brand is represented in marketing. While you can and should give guidelines about how you want your brand to be represented, <u>most influencers are creatives</u> who will want to put together their own posts. It's best to go back over paid posts and double check how you are being represented, so that you can give feedback.

Who's Using Influencers the Most

Most influencers represent brands that have physical, lifestyle products to sell, such as the beauty and fashion industry. This marketing is particularly useful for eCommerce sites to bring their products to life.
There are many budding uses of influencers both in the spheres of local and national business. Local influencers are also great representatives for local small

businesses, such as local grocery stores, specialty shops, and restaurants.

They can appeal to regional flavor and aesthetic, and easily relate to their audience. On the global side, influencer marketing can be similar to the affiliate marketing that is used by Amazon and various software and online brands. When it comes to software, influencers tend to appeal to a professional niche and post products to blogs.

2018 Influencer Trends to Look For

- Look for brands and influencers to be more transparent about their relationships. Sponsored posts should be marketed with a partner hashtag, i.e. #[BrandName]Partner.

- While Instagram is one of the main marketplaces for influencers, consider finding brand advocates on other platforms such as Facebook, Snapchat, Twitter, YouTube, and Pinterest. The pricing on these networks could be lower due to less traffic, and they could help you reach different, more personal audiences.

- Think about using an influencer marketing management tool like TapInfluence and Upfluence to help you organize and analyze this new marketing strategy.

- You can use specialized eCommerce codes and branded hashtags to track the ROI on influencers, so that you can better communicate with your target demographic.

Using your Natural Following

Your brand's natural following includes those people who already know what your brand has to offer. Sometimes they will already follow you on social media and email newsletters. If not, then invite them to do so. This following will already contain a warm market of brand advocates. These will be individuals who like your brand and mention it to their friends and family.

They might already be sharing your products and services on social media without compensation.

Cultivate this natural following by finding out what it likes, and how you can nurture it. Help them to develop a branded hashtag for you. Ask them to upload photos and videos of themselves using or wearing your product. Ask them to join the conversation, and always make sure to reply, credit, and engage.

In-House Influencers

Some brands are moving to hiring influencers onto their marketing team, or alternately, these brands are helping their employees to develop into influencers. Developing an in-house influencer team requires investments in education and training. However, the effort allows a strong sense of brand loyalty between the brand and the employee/influencer, as well as a sense of transparency about the brand itself.

Large brands, such as Hello Fresh, L'Occitane, and Birchbox are making the move toward internal influencer marketing teams. And while this is quickly becoming a trend among large companies, it has frequently been a practice among smaller businesses, as employees and brands link back and forth from personal to branded accounts about products, services, and accomplishments.

As you dive into the fun and interactive work of influencer marketing, keep in mind that your best scenario is to find an influencer who is loyal to your brand. This person should be a partner in your branding, and an advocate for your goods and services.

Conclusion

In this book, we've spent a lot of time showing you how to utilize social media in a different way. We've emphasized the importance of building a community, we've talked about initiating and maintaining relationships, and we've also shown you some very practical ways to get noticed.

We've also shared some stories of entrepreneurs like yourself that have built entire businesses on the back of social media marketing. You've read some of how StartUp Mindset has used social media to bring us to a place of authority and promise.

Now it's your turn. You must now decide if you are going to put this book down and think about what you've read or if you are going to take the step toward writing your own success story.

Whether you've been an entrepreneur for years or if you are still working a job and want to one day exercise your entrepreneurial potential, you have the opportunity to make an important decision. We hope you make the right choice.

ABOUT THE AUTHOR

StartUp Mindset is an entrepreneurship blog and media platform that was developed to help entrepreneurs and anyone else who wants to succeed in business. You'll find information, tools, resources, news and a ton of other goodies to spark your Startup mindset. In just a few years the site has grown and now reaches nearly 250,000 people per month through the blog and social media platforms. Visit the blog at Startupmindset.com

www.ingramcontent.com/pod-product-compliance
Lightning Source LLC
Chambersburg PA
CBHW052154220526
45471CB00004B/1674